SPIRITUAL FATHERHOOD

Evagrius Ponticus on the Role of the Spiritual Father

Spiritual Fatherhood

Evagrius Ponticus on the
Role of the Spiritual Father

Gabriel Bunge

Translated by
Luis Joshua Salés

ST VLADIMIR'S SEMINARY PRESS
YONKERS, NEW YORK
2016

Library of Congress Cataloging-in-Publication Data

Names: Bunge, Gabriel, 1940– author.
Title: Spiritual fatherhood : Evagrius Ponticus on the role of the spiritual
    father / Gabriel Bunge ; translated by Luis Joshua Salés.
Other titles: Geistliche Vaterschaft. English
Description: Yonkers : St Vladimirs Seminary Press, 2016. | Includes
    bibliographical references.
Identifiers: LCCN 2016037199 (print) | LCCN 2016037907 (ebook) | ISBN
    9780881415445 (alk. paper) | ISBN 9780881415452
Subjects: LCSH: Evagrius, Ponticus, 345?-399. | Fatherhood (Christian
    theology)--History of doctrines--Early church, ca. 30-600. | Gnosticism.
Classification: LCC BR65.E926 B8613 2016 (print) | LCC BR65.E926 (ebook) |
    DDC 230/.14--dc23
LC record available at https://lccn.loc.gov/2016037199

Translation copyright © 2016

ST VLADIMIR'S SEMINARY PRESS
575 Scarsdale Rd, Yonkers, NY 10707
1-800-204-2665
www.svspress.com

A translation of Gabriel Bunge, *Geistliche Vaterschaft.*
Eremos: Texte zur Spiritualität, Geschichte und Kunst,
herausgegeben von der Klause St. Benedikt, Band 1. Berlin: LIT Verlag. 2010

ISBN 978-0-88141-544-5 (paper)
ISBN 978-0-88141-545-2 (electronic)

Table of Contents

Spiritual Fatherhood—
An Outdated Subject?

Heed, O monk, your father's words,
and make not his admonitions fruitless.
Where he may send you, take him along,[1]
and with him go in thoughts.
In this way you surely will
flee from evil thoughts,
and wicked demons in no wise will
prevail against you.[2]

Fatherly images and fatherhood in the spiritual sense, as expressed in the beautiful text above (and recently, even in the physical sense) unmistakably entered into a serious crisis in the last decades of the past century. "Paternalism" is now a foul word. By now, something similar can even be said about the image of "mother." We live in a fatherless (and motherless) time that many, curiously, take as "liberation."

This "liberation" may have overcome some obsolete and outdated concept, but it has nevertheless left behind a certain void. As is common in such cases, things could not stay that way. Man cannot stand living in a void. So right away we introduced "substitute fathers" who promised to fill the gap. The political scene is not the only one populated by such "father figures."

Without intending to question the good intention of many of these "gurus" and father figures, we must still ask ourselves whether

[1] See Prov 6.20.
[2] *Mn* 73.

they measure up to their role. By the same token, there is good reason to suspect that those recently "liberated" have, in following these
"fathers," given themselves over, unawares, to a new, even stronger form
of dependence. In that case not much would be won, but rather much
would be lost, for in the spiritual realm the success of false father figures must be deemed tragic.

Tragic, since the point of true—and therefore also of "spiritual"—
fatherhood is precisely not dependence, either of the son on the father
or vice versa. The point of true fatherhood is much more about the
giving of life; it means allowing the other space for individual, free
being. The point of spiritual "sonhood" (since without it there can be
no "spiritual fatherhood") is free acceptance of this individual being as
being-related. "Father" and "son" are, regardless of the natural sex and
age of those involved, metaphors in the spiritual realm that express a
personal relationship. On this basis, tradition knows not only spiritual
"fathers," but also spiritual "mothers."

Since this same father-son image is also applied to the divine persons of the Holy Trinity, it is clear what is at stake, for one who lacks
the experience of true fatherhood and true sonship in the spiritual
realm is in danger of lacking any true personal experience of God.
The point of spiritual fatherhood is none other than the experience of
transcending one's own individuality in the encounter with an "other"
who bears the age-old name of "father," because in this transcendence
this other becomes the "begetter" of individual personhood. In the
absolute sense, the experience of becoming a person takes place solely
in the encounter with the "other" of God, whom, thanks to the Son in
the Holy Spirit, we may also call Abba, Father![3]

So, when the Christian tradition from early on ascribed the name
"father" to certain men (bishops, priests, and monks), although in the
gospel it says, "Call no one on earth your father, since your father is one,
the heavenly one,"[4] it could only mean that the spiritual fatherhood of
these men was the earthly means, as it were, through which the heavenly fatherhood of God was experienced. The experience of the former
leads to the experience of the latter. So, spiritual fatherhood fulfills its

[3]Rom 8.15.
[4]Mt 23.9.

role when the spiritual son comes to have "the measure of the stature of Christ,"[5] of the son in the absolute sense; that is, when he has made it all the way to true, personal experience of God.

The Christian tradition, given its firm grasp on the theological place of the spiritual experience of God, has never shied away from ascribing to certain "spiritually gifted" men and women the names *Abba* and *Amma*. This conviction is so central, and therefore so self-evident, that it is hardly ever called into question in the oldest monastic literature, making the following text from the Pachomian tradition all the more meaningful. It teaches, among other things, that cenobites and anchorites fully agreed with respect to this question, for we will find very similar sentiments in Evagrius.

The anonymous author of a *Life* of Pachomius takes as a starting point the Lord's words cited above: "Call no one on earth your father," which a few ignoramuses apparently used against the Pachomians' convention of calling Pachomius *apa*, father. The author points out that there are not only fathers on earth, that is, "in accordance with the flesh," but also certain others who, like Paul, "beget through the gospel in Christ Jesus."[6] It is true of them that "a man who 'begets' another in the work of God, is his father in accordance with God, in this world as much as in the coming one."

> This is reasonably the case for our father Pachomius, who has earned being called "father," since our Father who is in the heavens lives in him, as the apostle confesses with his mouth in saying: "I live not, rather Christ lives in me."[7] Therefore, all those who through their manner resemble the apostle have earned being called "father" on account of the Holy Spirit, who dwells in them.[8]

Here, in a nutshell, we have already all those elements that we will encounter in Evagrius: Men, whom we call "fathers," since they have become fathers to us "in accordance with God." As the citation

[5]Eph 4.13.
[6]1 Cor 5.15.
[7]Gal 2.20.
[8]L. T. Lefort, *Les vies coptes de Saint Pachôme et de ses premiers successeurs* (Löwen, 1943), 54f.

from Paul teaches, Christ is inferred by the phrase "Father, who is in the heavens." We will find this representation widespread in the early Church and quite familiar to every Benedictine from the prologue of the *Rule of Benedict*[9] and again in Evagrius.[10]

*

As the name indicates, spiritual fatherhood is a grace, an unattainable[11] gift of the Holy Spirit, not an institution. This charism is thus bound neither to the office nor to the sex and age of the one gifted. Here, of course, the question we will engage arises, namely, under what circumstances the Spirit imparts the charism of fatherhood to this or that person. No less important is the relationship between this charism of fatherhood, which is consistently conferred upon a few, and the spiritual gift of sonship that is conferred on all those baptized; this alone constitutes Christian existence.[12]

A backward glance at the early time of monasticism will prove to be extremely fruitful at this point. It will show that, far from being outdated, the topic of spiritual fatherhood is actually of utmost importance for us—although not in a trendy sense, since virtually everything "spiritual" today is very much in demand. Ultimately, true spiritual fatherhood is a touchstone that allows us more clearly to perceive and draw the borders between genuine mystic and mysticism, between true *gnosis* and false Gnosticism, than what is generally possible today. It acts very much like the foundational charism, but on a very different scale, of the institution that draws the line between Church and sect.

Finally, the relationship between the two charisms of spiritual fatherhood and that of the institution is also in vogue. A glance at the early history of monasticism shows that there were tensions as a matter of course; monks fled the institution especially when they were not possessed by a spirit of vainglory. For example, in the perspective of

---

[9]See B. Steidle, "Heilige Vaterschaft," *Benediktinische Monatsschrift* 14 (1932): 217ff.; id. "Abba-Vater," *ibid.* 16 (1934): 89–101; G. Racle, "A propos du Christ-Père," *RSR* (1962): 400–408 ; A. de Vogüé, "La paternité du Christ dans la Règle de Saint Benoît et du Maître," *La vie spirituelle* 110 (1964): 55–67.

[10]See below, chapter V.

[11][I.e., humanly unattainable, thus a grace.—*Ed.*]

[12]Cf. Rom 8.15; Gal 4.5; Eph 1.5.

their time Athanasius the Great and Antony the Great did not stand in opposition to each other—quite the opposite. In Evagrius' words it was the "wise" and the "wise of this world" who did.

Gregory of Nazianzus (called the Theologian) and the literarily uneducated Antony count for Evagrius as "righteous."[13] For him, the former and Macarius the Great are both "vessels of election,"[14] just as Paul before them,[15] since the bishop and the monastic father are both "Spirit-bearers,"[16] a term that is equally spiritually charged when applied to the one or the other. There is, however, nothing spiritual to be found in the words of reprobate persons regardless of who they are,[17] since "wisdom dwells not in a vicious heart, nor in a body that indulges sin."[18]

It is therefore certainly no coincidence that we attribute the Greek *Life* of Antony (which was to make Egyptian monasticism known far beyond its original confines—indeed, even in the West) to no one less than his very own bishop, Athanasius of Alexandria.

Therefore, it is immediately apparent that the charismatic-prophetic movement of monasticism and the charism of spiritual fatherhood that grew out of it have their place in the Church. This, however, means that spiritual fatherhood must have its place within the salvific economy of God, that is, that it participates in the Father's effecting of salvation in the Son through the Holy Spirit. The text from the Pachomian tradition cited above immediately hints at this. Thus, spiritual fatherhood is not a flight from God's breaking into history; on the contrary, it is one of those places wherein divine self-emptying can be experienced in a human way.

Such things have never been a problem for the Christian East, as the large number of spiritual fathers that it can point to even today demonstrates. It lives out that which today has become an issue for the

---

[13]*Pr Epil* 7; *Pr* 92.
[14]*Ep.fid.* 1.15; *Pr* 93.
[15]*Apg* 9.15.
[16]Cf. G.W. Lampe, *A Patristic Greek Lexicon* (Oxford, 1961), s.v. πνευματοφόρος, A 3.4; cf. *HL* 11: Butler 34.11 (Evagrius!).
[17]*Gn* 21.
[18]Wis 1.4.

largely scientifically determined, that is, rationally oriented, West. A serious backward glance to the resources of the early era (upon which the spirituality of the Christian East is still nourished) may help us to uncover the roots of some of the symptoms of malnutrition complained about, as well as of many imported, substitute solutions, so that we may find the way back to the spirit of the early fathers.[19]

---

[19]Cf. G. Bunge, *Auf den Spuren der Heiligen Väter*, Weisungen der Väter 1 (Beuron, 2007).

CHAPTER I

In the Spirit of the "Holy Fathers"

Perhaps someone will inquire here why we should take a "desert father," of all people, as a mentor—especially this barely known, not to mention somewhat controversial, Evagrius of Pontus (*c.* 345–399).[1] There are several reasons. Evagrius, who beginning around 383 lived and wrote in the Nitrian desert, and thereafter in the even more secluded "Kellia," is, from a literary standpoint, among the oldest witnesses to the spirituality of the desert fathers.

Moreover, Macarius the Great and Macarius the Alexandrian, two of the most respected spiritual fathers of their time, were among his mentors.[2] Macarius the Great also knew Antony the Great, and word had it his "spirit" had passed on to him.[3] In other words, the writings of Evagrius afford us authentic access to a particular spirituality that goes back to the "firstfruits of the anchorites,"[4] Antony the Great.[5]

Antony, whom incidentally the Pachomians themselves reverently called "our holy father *apa* Antonius,"[6] regarded himself as father of the young monastic communities that had cropped up under his influence;[7] he was also regarded by the others as such.[8] Not only did he exercise this spiritual fatherhood through the spoken word, but he

---

[1]Concerning Evagrius, his life and work, cf. G. Bunge, *Evagrios Pontikos: Briefe aus der Wüste* (Trier, 1985).

[2]Cf. G. Bunge, "Évagre le Pontique et les deux Macaire," *Irénikon* 56 (1983): 215–227, 323–360.

[3]*HM* 21.2.

[4]*M.c.* 25.27.

[5]Cf. S. Rubenson, "Evagrios Pontikos und die Theologie der Wüste," in F. L. Abrahamowski, H. C. Brennecke, et al., *LOGOS* (Berlin, 1993), 384–401.

[6]L. Th. Lefort, *Les vies coptes de Saint Pachôme et de ses premiers successeurs* (Löwen, 1943), 79.6.

[7]*Vita Antonii* 15.3; 16.2.

[8]*L.c.* 54.6.

also extended his contact in written form, as his seven authentic letters attest. Their teaching is related in many ways to that of Evagrius.

Thus, we may with some justification hope to find in Macarius the Great's[9] undoubtedly most famous student not only a very much thought-out, but also an especially original teaching of spiritual fatherhood, particularly since his contemporaries were full of wonder at his fine and even-handed judgment in spiritual matters.[10] If Evagrius, for the modern researcher, is first and foremost a "philosopher in the desert,"[11] he was exactly the same in the opinion of the ancients, in early Christianity's sense of "philosopher": "As Evagrius became a student (of the two Macarii) he acquired philosophy through works, noticing that he had long been a philosopher in speech."[12]

Already while in Constantinople Evagrius did not strive after the "wisdom coming from without"[13] and belonging to the Hellenes,[14] but rather after the "highest philosophy"[15]—that is, for Christianity, understood as "the teaching of Christ, our Redeemer."[16] Yet not until he received the guidance of the "holy fathers" did that scion, which the "righteous Gregory" had planted in him at that time, grow into a vine, from whose fruits we still eat today.[17] The "philosopher through works" became, like Macarius the Great—whom Evagrius calls his "holy and most experienced" (*praktikōtatos*) teacher[18]—a man who in a single élan links the search for an accomplished moral life with the search for godly wisdom. In the following depiction Evagrius certainly was not thinking of himself, although his contemporaries would have readily recognized him in it.[19]

---

[9]*HM* (Rufinus), 27 (7.2).

[10]*HM* (Rufinus), 27 (7.1).

[11]Cf. A. Guillaumont, "Un philosophe au désert: Évagre le Pontique," *RHR* 181 (1972): 29–56. The major synthesis of the late scholar appeared in Paris in 2004, also under the same title.

[12]Sokrates, *HE* 4.23.34.

[13]*Ep.fid.* 2.5.

[14]*Ant* 7.37.

[15]*Ep.fid.* 1.14.

[16]*Pr* 1.

[17]*Pr* 1.

[18]*Pr* 29.

[19]Cf. *HM* 20.15–16; *HM* (Rufinus) 27.

Praiseworthy is the man who links together praxis and gnosis, in order to water from both springs the field of the soul, particularly with regard to virtue. For the gnostic "gives wings"[20] to intelligible being, i.e., the intellect, through the contemplation of better things, whereas praxis "kills the earthly members, fornication, impurity, passion, malice, wicked coveting."[21] Those, therefore, who through these two are clad as if with armor,[22] will easily trample underfoot the wickedness of demons.[23]

A thoroughly thought-out synthesis that proceeds from the salvific realities of revelation[24] and joins together the practical, i.e., the practice of the gospel virtues, with the theoretical or gnostic, i.e., contemplative knowledge of creation and its Maker, is possibly the most original contribution of the Pontic monk to ancient monastic spirituality. The object of this synthesis that consisted in the practical and gnostic was quite concrete: it was necessary to bar the way to the temptation of pseudo-gnosis spreading at that time in monastic circles.[25]

Ultimately, the lasting value of Evagrius does not lie in this achievement, for the only practicable answer to the challenge of modern pseudo-gnosis—which today increasingly trickles down to widening layers of the intelligentsia, as well as to the common folk—is a true Christian *gnosis*, as it already was at the time of Clement and Origen, and indeed, at the very time of the Evangelist John or the Apostle Paul. Its basis is not vain human curiosity and wild speculative craving, but the faith that extends throughout life toward the knowledge of the mysteries of the revelation encompassed in it.

"As we have heard it, so also have we seen it, in the city of the Lord of hosts, in the city of our God":[26] What we hear about

[20]For the Platonic image of the "wings" (of knowledge) see *KG* II.6; 2 *in Ps* 54.7; *M.c.* 29. Cf. also G. Bunge, *Das Geistgebet* (Köln, 1987), Chapter V.
[21]Cf. Col 3.5.
[22]Cf. Eph 6.11, 13.
[23]Eul 15.
[24]Cf. *Ep.fid.* 4!
[25]Cf. G. Bunge, "Origenismus-Gnostizismus. Zum geistesgeschichtlichen Standort des Evagrios Pontikos," *Vigiliae Christianae* 40 (1986): 24–54.
[26]Ps 47.9. [The psalms are regularly cited according to the Septuagint numbering.—*Ed.*]

God through faith,[27] that we know through a pure life, in that we accept[28] the "proofs"[29]of what is believed through dispassion.

In contradistinction to any form of ancient or modern pseudo-gnosis, the Johannine and Pauline "knowledge" (gnosis) is not the *way* to salvation, but the *fruit* of the salvation accepted in faith. It is not the result of arbitrary speculations nor of alleged (and frequently also expensively purchased) "initiations," but the unattainable gifts of grace of God to those who have undertaken the effort of seriously following Christ. Thus, its content is no more than those salvific realities that become accessible to all the baptized through faith. Christian mysticism is thus ultimately nothing other than internalized theology.

What makes this "true knowledge"—even that of Evagrius—appear foreign to the outsider is the fact that an internalized knowledge has an entirely different radiance, a very different intensity, than has a mere rationally grasped truth. The former remains, so to speak, surrounded by a veil of unknowing which only dissipates when one "has become" this truth (Meister Eckhart). Then it awakens marvel, astonishment, and a joyful hymn.

The *Letter to Melania* is a moving testimony from Evagrius' stylus with regard to this process of internalization.[30] That the Logos "became man" in his body "so that man might become God" is known to every believer. But when the mystic enters inside this salvific reality, he becomes so enraptured with awe at the enormity of this salvific gift that he, as in this case, is no longer able to complete the original intention of his letter.

Every believer knows also that "God is love"[31] and that "he wills that all men be saved and come to the knowledge of the truth."[32] Yet, the mystic who enters within this truth collapses physically under the load of the sweetness of this knowledge. He becomes as if mad and

---

[27]Cf. Rom 10.17.
[28]Cf. 1 Cor 2.4.
[29]5 *in Ps* 47.9.
[30]Cf. Bunge, *Briefe*, 303ff.
[31]1 Jn 4.8, 16.
[32]1 Tim 2.4.

goes about his day in thoroughly unusual, even foolish, behavior, as the great Syrian mystic Jausep Hazzaya describes it rather movingly.[33]

*

At all times, and not only in Christianity, the "master" plays a rather particular role on the road to ethical perfection and in the search for godly wisdom. On this road forward, the role of "leader" frequently falls to the "student." In the Christian context, the idea of spiritual fatherhood developed here and has endured in full bloom up to the present day, particularly in the Christian East.

But Gnosticism also endures in full bloom up to the present day; and at that, it endures significantly and most notably in the very West. Its "teachers" and "initiates" promise knowledge and insight into "eternal truth." How can one tell what is real from what is false? The study of Evagrius, one of the great figures of early monasticism, whom Henry Chadwick rightly called the "father of our spiritual literature,"[34] can prove helpful here.

First, we can learn from Evagrius that the matter of the struggle with Gnosticism—which is as old as Christianity itself, if not older—is done a disservice whenever we avoid the questions and terminology that Gnosticism has coopted. That also goes for the central term "gnosis" itself. The idea of the "knowledge" (of God and his mysteries) plays a rather essential role in the books of the New Testament, specifically in John and Paul. The word "gnosis" at that point was not yet negatively charged, particularly since in the first place it means simply "knowledge," without any preconceptions. In order to distinguish true from false knowledge, Paul coins the phrase "falsely so-called knowledge" (*pseudonymos gnosis*).[35]

The same goes for him upon whom this "knowledge" has been bestowed. Paul touts the ideal of the "spiritually gifted,"[36] and John that of the "discerning."[37] Following Clement of Alexandria

---

[33]Cf. G. Bunge, *Rabban Jausep Hazzaya, Briefe über das geistliche Leben und verwandte Schriften* (Trier: Paulinus-Verlag, 1982).

[34]O. Chadwick, *John Cassian* (Cambridge, 1968), 86.

[35]1 Tim 6.20.

[36]1 Cor 2.13, 15.

[37]1 John passim.

here,[38] Evagrius speaks, unperturbed, about the "gnostic," a term which was not foreign to him as a Greek. The word designates simply a person who "was reckoned worthy of knowledge"[39] by God—that is to say, of course, of the "true knowledge."

Incidentally, the term "Gnostic" is also significantly less charged than we commonly assume. Apparently, only as of the eighteenth century[40] do we designate by the term "Gnostic" an adherent of the error stigmatized by Paul as "pseudo-gnosis." Insofar as we speak generally of "gnosis," regrettably, we have surrendered an originally Christian field to this error, without a fight. To counteract that, in recent times the convention of applying the term "Gnosticism" to "pseudo-gnosis" has gained acceptance, in order to distinguish it from "gnosis" in the Christian sense. In what follows, we use the words "gnosis" and "Gnostic" in the biblical and patristic sense.

Incidentally, the same goes for "wisdom," that ancient ideal of humanity to which some of the most beautiful books of the Old Testament are devoted. Here, too, a differentiation is necessary. In this respect, Evagrius opposes the "wisdom" of God to the "external"—"the wisdom coming from without" (or knowledge)[41]—and provides criteria that enable its differentiation. His "wise man" or "gnostic" is the man who does not owe his wisdom and knowledge to simple study, but possesses them as gifts of the grace of God.[42]

This already indicates that the spiritual father, through whom divine wisdom "begets many through virtue and the knowledge of God,"[43] must be understood on the basis of his internal relationship to God alone, who is "essential wisdom."[44] So, as previously indicated, the theological locus of spiritual fatherhood is faith in the God of biblical revelation, who freely communicates himself to men—or to the Church, more precisely, which received this revelation and passes it on alive. Therefore, spiritual fatherhood is one of the charisms of the Holy Spirit, which is conferred inside the mystery of the "Church" alone.

[38] Cf A. and C. Guillaumont in their edition of the *Gnostikos*, 24ff.
[39] So the turn of phrase that is also found in the title of the *Gnostikos*.
[40] Cf. Lampe, l.c. s.v.
[41] 37 *in Ps* 118.85.
[42] Gen 4.45.
[43] *Ep* 52.7.
[44] *KG* 1.89.

CHAPTER II

Evagrius as Spiritual Son of the Holy Fathers

No one can be someone else's spiritual father before he himself has been a spiritual son. Even the case of Antony the Great, who was father of the monks and "firstfruits of the anchorites,"[1] was no different. Before he retreated to the desert, he sought and found advice from an old ascetic[2] who, for his part, could have been related in one way or another to that asceticism of the early church that chronologically precedes monasticism. Before we study the Evagrian teaching on spiritual fatherhood, it will be helpful to turn our attention to the life of the monk Evagrius. How did he himself live that which he later taught to others?

Although he was himself—not only for the sake of his writings, but also for the sake of the instruction of his contemporaries—a reclusive Abba[3] in high demand, Evagrius remained a lifelong obedient pupil of the elders. Just as at one point Gregory of Nazianzus "planted" him,[4] so also the holy fathers in the desert "watered" him through their instructions[5]—or so the story goes, in a relatively old text.

We know through his friend Rufinus and other contemporaries[6] that Evagrius was the student of the two Macarii. According to Palladius, at the beginning of Evagrius' life in the desert, Macarius the Alexandrian, who was the priest of the monastic colony at Kellia, gave

[1]Evagrius calls him so, *M.c.* 35.
[2]*Vita Antonii* 3.3.
[3]Macarius the Alexandrian, the priest of Kellia, also calls him so in the Apophthegmata of *Evagrius* 7.
[4]*Ep* 46; cf. 1 Cor 3.6.
[5]*Pr Epil* 7ff.
[6]Rufinus, *HM* 27 (7.2); Socrates, *HE* 4.23.34.

him a rule for living—incidentally, one far too rigorous for the spoiled and cultured Greeks—in order to tame his overly passionate nature. Evagrius observed it faithfully for years until he became seriously ill. As a result, the older fathers (Macarius had already died by 390) prescribed him a milder rule that he observed for the last two years of his life, up to his death in 399.[7] We also find out through Palladius that he found a close confidant in the affluent Roman Albinus (perhaps a relative of Melania the Elder, who played such a decisive role[8] in his monastic call), to whom he could turn for advice in times of internal need.[9]

These testimonies of close confidants are fully confirmed by Evagrius himself. In this vein, he casually reports his visit to Macarius the Alexandrian, a rigorous ascetic.[10] He sought John of Lykopolis, the seer of Thebes; to this end, he had to undertake a toilsome journey of more than two weeks to discuss with him extremely subtle questions about the mystical life.[11] We also see him in conversation with Macarius of Egypt;[12] to that end, he had to hike through the desert from Kellia to the far distant Sketis. He regarded Macarius the Great, whom he placed side by side with his former teacher Gregory of Nazianzus, in the honor of "highest philosophy." Macarius was his lifelong spiritual teacher par excellence.

Based on the way he quotes him, we can conclude that Evagrius personally knew Didymus the Blind as well.[13] Antony the Great repeatedly visited Didymus in his cell on an island in Lake Mareotis[14] in the proximity of Alexandria. Evagrius must have really revered the elder, who was highly regarded in his time; he appears to owe important insights to him. His own student Palladius also visited Didymus repeatedly,[15] not unlike Jerome, who would later disown him.

---

[7]*Vita* C; *HL* 38: Butler 122.8ff.

[8]*Vita* 11, cf. G. Bunge and A. de Vogüé, *Quatre ermites égyptiens* (Bellefontaine, 1994), 173–175.

[9]*HL* 38: Butler 119.10ff. Cf. Bunge, *Briefe*, 29ff.

[10]*Pr* 94.

[11]*Ant* 6.16; compare to the proximate circumstances with *HL* 35.

[12]*Pr* 93.

[13]*Pr* 98. Cf. *Gn* 48.

[14]*HL* 4: Butler 20.6–8.

[15]*HL* 4: Butler 19.18–21.

*

Besides many other unnamed fathers, not only should we honor[16] these holy fathers or elders "as the angels" on account of their words, but we should also explore their ways so as to distort not even slightly the true spirit of monasticism.[17] "For much that is beautiful is found that was said and done by them."[18] Evagrius therefore never fails in his own writings to rely on the living witness or the words of the older fathers, which next to the Scriptures constitute the basis of the spiritual life. Indeed, he even asserts in his *Praktikos* that he faithfully transmits nothing more than the teaching of the fathers insofar as is appropriate for general dissemination.[19]

Evagrius references Antony the Great,[20] with whose *Life* and *Seven Letters* he evidently was familiar; Macarius the Egyptian[21] and his namesake, the Alexandrian;[22] Didymus the Blind;[23] John of Lykopolis[24] and John the Little,[25] as well as Theodore of Tabennesi,[26] with whose *Life* (in an earlier Greek version, no longer extant) he must have been familiar. Thanks to Palladius, we can add to the list the highly cultured Ammonius Parotes, whose ascetical perfection dazzled Evagrius considerably,[27] and Albinus,[28] famous on account of his meekness. Thanks to the *Apophthegmata*, we can also add the affluent Roman Arsenius.[29]

There are many unnamed "gnostic"[30] or "thoroughgoing practical"[31] fathers besides these, in whose company Evagrius himself experienced

[16]*Pr* 100.
[17]*Ep* 17.1.
[18]*Pr* 91.
[19]*Pr Prol* [8] [9].
[20]*Ant* 4.47; *Pr* 92; *M.c.* 35.
[21]*Ant* 4.45; *Pr* 29.93; *Or* Prol.
[22]*Ant* 4.23.48; 8.26; *Pr* 94; *M.c.* 37.
[23]*Gn* 48; *Pr* 98; *Ep* 59.3 (?).
[24]*Ant* 2.36; 5.6; 6.16; 7.19; *Or* 73 (?).
[25]*Or* 107.
[26]*Or* 108.
[27]*HL* 11: Butler 34.11f.; cf. Socrates *HE* 4.23.75–76; cf. also *Ant* 6.16.
[28]*HL* 35: Butler 101.5 (apparatus); 47: Butler 137.9.
[29]*Arsenios* 5. Evagrius' name is attested through the Syriac and Latin translation.
[30]*Gn* 3.5, etc.
[31]*Pr* 29.

what spiritual fatherhood means. The figure of the spiritual father that coincides with the "gnostic," as we encounter it in Evagrius' writings, is in no way an idealization foreign to reality or a simple construct; rather, it is a trustworthy reflection of a reality lived out.

*

The picture painted by this overview speaks for itself. Evagrius shows us a cultured Greek in full possession of the philosophical and theological culture of his time. In his mature age he betakes himself to the schools of the great spiritual masters and mystics of Egyptian monasticism, who were frequently simple Copts without Hellenic culture.

This harmonious alliance between two worlds only superficially opposed to each other (an alliance unmistakably fruitful for both sides) is manifestly characteristic of the anchoritic form of early Egyptian monasticism. It has tradition as it were. We think of the "uncultured" Antony,[32] in the Greek sense of culture, and his preferred student, Serapion, later bishop of Thmuis and one of the most cultured men of his time.[33] In the following generation we also think of Pambo, who was incompetent in reading,[34] and of his student Ammonius, whose extensive theological and biblical culture his contemporaries extolled.[35]

The first Origenist crisis (399–403) of ignominious memory,[36] which wreaked havoc on the spiritual realm, would have consequences no less catastrophic than the material devastation of Sketis at the hands of the nomadic Mazacians (407/8). It is well known that Evagrius' memory

[32]In reality there are indeed two fathers named Antony. We encounter the better known in a *Life* by the stylus of Athanasius the Great. Here, Antony appears above all as a great ascetic, albeit not missing "contemplative" traits. Many apophthegmata were composed in this spirit. The lesser known Antony is the one of the letters, whom we also encounter in testimonies from his "school," as, say, in Evagrius (*Pr* 92) and Cassian (*Conf* 9.31). This Antony is quite inspired by Alexandrian theology, albeit one can notice his lack of "professionalization in the discipline" at every turn. Cf. S. Rubenson, "The Letters of Saint Antony," in *Origenist Theology: Monastic Tradition and the Making of a Saint* (Lund, 1990 and Minneapolis, 1995) with a translation of the seven letters.

[33]Cf. R. Draguet, "Une lettre de Sérapion de Thmuis aux disciples d'Antoine (A.D. 356)," *Le Muséon* 64 (1951): 1–25.

[34]Cf. Bunge and de Vogüé, *Quatre ermites égyptiens*, 95.

[35]*HL* 11: Butler 34.5–9.

[36]Cf. Bunge, *Briefe* 54ff.

and work were very much harmed by reason of the ill-willed distrust of the "cultured monks" (*logiōteroi*) that engendered this crisis, which was essentially motivated by church politics. This distrust has made a factual appraisal of his teaching difficult even today.

It seems to us that the rupture between "spirituality" and "theology" began with this first Origenist crisis, a rupture that with greater or lesser intensity runs like a red thread through Church history until finally—in the West, in any case—it results in a nearly complete break.[37] The consequences today are unmistakable. "Spirituality" (whatever we understand by it) has disengaged "theology" from dogma to such a degree that it was able to open itself to the manifold Far Eastern "mystics" (often blended with the manifold mutations of ancient Gnosticism), without eliciting any appreciable protest.

And so it happens that today many believe one thing (or think they still believe) and practice another.[38] In other words, that happy synthesis of the practical and the contemplative that Evagrius had worked out, was lost. Given that this is the case, it could only follow that the true spiritual fatherhood regarded as indispensable in the contemplative monasticism of old is also missing, and all manner of "teachers" have an easy job with those who are searching. Indeed, better knowledge of the life and work of the great mystic Evagrius will not remedy the deficiency, but may perhaps indicate the way back to the sources, for *knowing* without *doing* accomplishes nothing—or only a little.

---

[37]In the Christian East, hesychasm still constitutes an efficient counterbalance.

[38]Cf. G. Bunge, *Irdene Gefäße: Die Praxis des persönlichen Gebetes nach der Überlieferung der heiligen Väter* (Würzburg, 1999).

CHAPTER III

Abba Evagrius

Although he was a lifelong obedient pupil of the holy fathers, Evagrius himself soon became a spiritual father in great demand and the widely read author of spiritual writings. Incidentally, in his own life this inevitably earned him the envy of his less sought-after brothers. Nevertheless, such undisputed "greats" as his master Macarius the Great and John Kolobos did not themselves escape this perennial *invidia clericalis*.[1] Palladius, who let himself boast that he had had Evagrius as a teacher[2] and owed him[3] his initiation into the "life in Christ," as well as a spiritual understanding of the Holy Scriptures, left us a lively image of the function of Evagrius as a spiritual father.

His custom was the following: The brothers would gather around him on Saturday and Sunday. All night long they discussed their thoughts with him. They harkened to his powerful words until the light came up. Then they departed thence full of happiness and praised God. For his instruction was truly very pleasant.

When they came to him, then he asked them and spoke: "My brothers, when one among you has a deep or a painful thought, then he should keep quiet until the other brothers have withdrawn, and then he may ask freely when there are just the two of us. In this way we do not speak before the brothers so that no 'little one' becomes undone through his thoughts or so that the pain (of the heart) likewise not devour him."

He was also so hospitable that he accepted five to six strangers daily in his cell, who came to him away from home in order to hear

---

[1]*HL* 27: Butler 81.4ff. (Heron); *HL syr.* [73.4] (Eucarpius).
[2]*HL* 23: Butler 75.5.
[3]*Vita* Ab.

his instruction, his understanding, and his asceticism. For he had at his disposal (necessary) money, given that many sent him some, so that he had more than 200 silver pieces that were deposited with his administrator, who constantly served in his dwelling.[4]

Rufinus, who was another confidant of the father of monks, has left behind in the shorter but no less revealing account in his Latin treatment, the *Historia Monachorum in Aegypto*, the impression Evagrius had on his visitors.

> We saw there (in Kellia) also a wholly and in every regard astonishing man, Evagrius by name. Besides other virtues of the Spirit, he was granted such a grace of "discernment of spirits" and the purification of thoughts, as the apostle says,[5] that it was felt that no brother had yet come to such a knowledge of psychological and spiritual matters.
>
> Although he had collected this great insight through study and personal experience and, what is even greater, through God's grace, one must yet add that he was taught for a long time by the blessed Macarius [the Great], who is a man distinguished in the highest measure by God's grace as well as by signs and wonders.[6]

Evagrius linked to these inordinate gifts a deep humility of the heart at which we still wonder in his writings today, and which surely did not just come to him; it is all the more remarkable in the formerly proud deacon of the bishop of Constantinople.[7]

> In his character he was granted modesty, with which he subjugated conceit and pride so much that he neither became boastful at deserved applause, nor resentful at the abuse of unjustified reproach.[8]

---

[4]*Vita* E–F.
[5]I Cor 12.10.
[6]*HM* (Rufinus) 27 (7.1–2). Some concrete ascetical instructions follow, which Evagrius gave to his visitors from Jerusalem on the way.
[7]*HL* 38: Butler 119.14ff.
[8]Sozomenos, *HE* 6.30.7. Cf. Bunge, *Letters Briefe* 78ff.; *Vita* K–L; *Gn* 32.

According to the reliable witness of his student and biographer Palladius, Evagrius owed his insight into the unique worth of modesty to a mysterious experience; he made it the center of his ascetical teaching in the form of meekness (*praotēs*).[9]

One time the spirit of blasphemy reviled him,[10] and he spent forty days (in the open), without going under the roof of a cell, until his body was entirely covered with bugs, like that of a mindless beast.[11]

After a few days he shared with us the revelation that he had seen, and that he never concealed from his students. He said: "It happened as I was sitting with a burning lamp in my cell at night. I was meditating about one of the prophets. In the middle of the night I was (suddenly) enraptured and found myself as if in a dream during sleep. I saw myself suspended in the air, (elevated) as far as the clouds and I took in the entire world [with one glance]. And the one to whom I was clinging said to me: "Do you see all this?" To be clear, he had elevated me into the clouds, and I saw the entire world at once. I said to him: "Yes." Then he said to me: "I will give you an order. If you keep it, you will be the ruler over everything you see.[12] Thereafter he said to me: "Go, be merciful and meek[13] and place your thought sincerely on God[14] and you will be the ruler over all of this." And no sooner had he said this that I found myself again with the book in hand and the wick of the lamp burning. And I did not know how I had been elevated up to the clouds, whether in the flesh, I do not know, God knows it, whether in spirit, I do not know.[15]

[9]Cf. Bunge, *Letters Briefe*.

[10]This temptation is typical for the demon of pride. Cf. *Ant* 8; *Pr* 43; 46; 51.

[11]Cf. *HL* 38: Butler 121.5–9. The rest is unique to the "longer version." [For this, see Tim Vivian, ed., *Four Desert Fathers,* Popular Patristics Series, No. 27 (Crestwood, NY: St. Vladimir's Seminary Press, 2004), pp. 85–87.—*Ed.*]

[12]"To rule" means "know," here, creation, cf. 8 *in Ps* 44.10; 1 *in Ps* 113.1–2; 6 to *in Ps* 134.12; *in Prov* 1.2: Géhin 3.

[13]Literally, "humble." As the sequence and the citation from Ps 24:9 show, in Greek the discussion was about "meekness."

[14]Cf. *Gn* 42, 43; 5 *in Ps* 143.7.

And so he fought for these two virtues, as if (with them) he would possess all virtues. And he said: "Meekness leads the spirit to correct knowledge, which pulls it upward."[16] For it is written: "He will teach the meek his ways."[17] For this virtue is that of the angels.[18] As concerns the purity of the body: "Monks and virgins are not the only ones who possess it, for they (admittedly) possess this virtue, but there are also many among the laity who preserve purity."[19]

From this experience, which clearly shocked him deeply, Evagrius draws the conclusion: "Seek peace with all and sanctification, without which no one will see the Lord,"[20] i.e., that inner and outer peace, of which he speaks so movingly in his *Treatise for the Monk Eulogios*,[21] and "sanctification" as the goal of the "practical" life, without which no one will arrive at the vision of God.[22] Palladius testifies explicitly that Evagrius took the heavenly man's advice seriously and made it the routine of his life, and that he ultimately also became a participant of the promise bound with the order: "After he had purified his intellect in the highest degree in the course of fifteen years, he was made worthy of the gifts of knowledge, wisdom, and discernment."[23]

With this gift of the "discernment of spirits" is implied not only a precise knowledge of demons and the passions they fan into flame, but also, as another episode from the life of Evagrius shows[24] and to which he himself later alludes once,[25] the discernment of truth from falsehood with respect to the faith. We will see that this particular

[15]Cf. 2 Cor 12.2!

[16]Cf. *Ep* 36.3. For the relationship between meekness and knowledge, cf. Bunge, *Letters Briefe* 126ff.

[17]Ps 24.9. Evagrius quotes this verse repeatedly, cf. *Ep* 56.3; *M.c.* 13, and comments on it as follows: "When someone wants to know the 'ways of the Lord,' let him become meek, since it is written: He will teach the meek his ways. . . ." (*3 in Ps* 24.4).

[18]Concerning meekness as the virtue of angels, cf. *Pr* 76; *KG* 4.38.

[19]*Vita* J–K.

[20]Heb 12.14.

[21]*Eul* 6.

[22]*Pr Prol* [8], cf. Bunge, *Letters Briefe* 118ff.

[23]*HL* 38: Butler 120.12–14.

[24]*HL* 38: Butler 121.9ff. and extensively *Vita* O.11 (11).

[25]*Mn* 126. Cf. Bunge, "Origenismus-Gnostizismus."

discernment of spirits belongs to the most primordial tasks of the spiritual father as teacher of "true knowledge."[26]

Palladius, who was familiar with Evagrius' living conditions by virtue of his own longstanding contact with him, does not ascribe to his teacher the gift of miracle-working by mistake. By this gift the great fathers had already distinguished themselves in the spirit of the age. Later people, such as the historian Socrates, noted this characteristic trait: "Many wondrous signs likewise happened through his hands, as through those of his (two) teachers [Macarius the Great and Macarius the Alexandrian]."[27]

A part of these wondrous deeds is not only "signs," such as the opening of a locked door whose key had been lost, through a simple sign of the cross,[28] but also averting others from error, which falls to the spiritual father. Thus, Palladius not only notes that his teacher kept him from the deception of pseudo-gnosis,[29] but he also reports the wondrous healing of the wife of a tribune during a sojourn in Palestine. This woman had openly given herself over to teachings of the Manicheans, who are decidedly the enemies of the body and creation, and had given up her marital union with her husband. Evagrius healed her "through a single word and a single prayer"[30] from the blindness of a simple "external wisdom."[31]

We can conclude on the basis of these direct and indirect testimonies that Evagrius, who throughout his life personally considered himself unworthy to lead others,[32] must have been a gifted spiritual father of rare charisma, on par with his own teachers. His teaching, therefore, bears the seal of quality of his own life.

---

[26]*In Prov* 30.4: Géhin 282B, 283; *idem* 6.30–31: Géhin 84.

[27]Sokrates, *HE* 4.23.35.

[28]*HL* 38: Butler 122.1–4.

[29]*Vita* Ab. Cf. Bunge, "Origenismus-Gnostizismus."

[30]*Vita* M.

[31]Concerning this "external wisdom" and the philosophers who represent it, cf. *KG* 1.73; 5 *in Ps* 48.11; 2 *in Ps* 62.4; 37 *in Ps* 118.85; *Gn* 4.

[32]*Ep* 9.1; 49.2. Cf. also *Ep* 13.1–2; 26; 50.1–2; 58.5.

CHAPTER IV
Spiritual Fatherhood: A Sketch

Based on this summary portrait of Evagrius, we see the contours of the figure of the spiritual father emerging in the same way that the Pontic monk experienced them in others, and himself lived them out. The spiritual father is first and foremost a man who has subjected himself to long years of the toils of asceticism—the praxis, as Evagrius says, of carrying out the commandments[1]—and has become an "eminently experienced"[2] monk. "Praxis" is that "spiritual method that purifies the passionate part of the soul"[3] and grants access to that "practical knowledge"[4] that allows one henceforth "to devote oneself to praxis with knowledge."[5] We cannot teach others what we have not lived out. That is more or less what the following commentary on a verse of the Psalms says:

> "There does the sparrow nest his young": He who through wakefulness and asceticism has become a "sparrow,"[6] he [himself] is also able to become the father of the "young."[7]

The fruit of the collaboration of divine grace and human effort[8] is dispassion (*apatheia*), that is, freedom from the tyranny of the passions understood as a natural "health of the soul"[9]—since in fact all evil, in

---

[1] *Pr* 81.
[2] *Pr* 29.
[3] *Pr* 78.
[4] 72 *in Ps* 118.159.
[5] *Pr* 50.
[6] Ps 101.8, cf. *Ep* 56.8.
[7] 15 *in Ps* 103.17.
[8] Cf. 12 *in Ps* 17.21; *KG* 1.79.
[9] *Pr* 56.

comparison to the original creaturely state, is like a disease[10]—invariably ontologically "secondary."[11]

Only the know-how attained through personal experience (when God additionally bestows upon him the gift of the "discernment of spirits") makes the monk a man "eminently experienced in the ascetical life,"[12] who is then also reliably able to indicate to others the "way of praxis."[13]

*

The outstanding virtue of such a man is love (*agapē*), the "offshoot of dispassion"[14] and the actual "goal of the practic."[15] Love is a multivalent word. For Evagrius, to be sure, it invariably takes a very specific form, since it manifests itself as a certain meekness (*praotēs*). According to the witness of the Scriptures, meekness was the most prominent quality of Moses,[16] David,[17] and Christ himself.[18] Based on these three supreme exemplars, we may take meekness as a form of love that prompts those who possess it not to dominate the other, but to give him space for individual being, even to the point of self-abandonment.[19] This meekness expresses itself in particular as discretion in dealing with others; it expresses itself as a loving foray into the needs and ability of the other who asks for advice.

Meek love, however, is not only the "goal of the practic," but also a "door of the knowledge of created nature,"[20] whose only "goal is knowledge of God himself."[21] "Knowledge" and "wisdom," then, are certain charisms of the Holy Spirit, which Evagrius invariably designates as

[10] *KG* 1.41.
[11] *KG* 1.40; *Ep* 59.3.
[12] *Pr* 29.
[13] 14 *in Ps* 118.32.
[14] *Pr* 81.
[15] *Pr* 84.
[16] Num 12.3.
[17] Ps 131.1.
[18] Mt 11.29.
[19] *Ep* 56.
[20] *Pr Prol* [8].
[21] *Mn* 3.

"spiritual," and which God grants only to those whom he has found worthy of them.

Spiritual fatherhood also belongs to these charisms, whose primordial goal is to rear others in the way of praxis "by means of virtue and, through its instruction, by means of the knowledge of God."[22] The ideals of the "gnostic" and the "wise" converge here with the ideal of the "master."

But before we turn to these various aspects in particular, the next task is to define more precisely the historically salvific and theological place of this spiritual fatherhood. The fact that we are dealing here with an unattainable charism of the Holy Spirit clearly indicates that the expression "spiritual father" applied to Evagrius is not a matter of just the title—that is to say, he is not the head of a "school" or "sect" in the manner of the philosophical schools of antiquity or of the non-Christian religions. Rather, he assumes a specific place in that particular human history led by God, which we call "salvation history," for salvation happens here, in history.

---

[22] *Ep* 52.7.

CHAPTER V

Christ as "Father" and Spiritual Fatherhood

As we saw at the beginning, the Pachomians who called their founder *apa* (father) traced this usage back to the fatherhood of Christ.[1] The student experiences the divine fatherhood of Christ very concretely through obedience to the "spiritual father." Calling Christ "father"—something surely unfamiliar to modern sensitivities—was rather common in the ancient Church; all Benedictines encounter it even today in the prologue of the *Rule of St Benedict*. Evagrius too is familiar with it—but how does he understand this fatherhood of Christ and in what relationship does it stand to spiritual fatherhood?

It is all the more fitting for us to expect the fruits of love from you, the fruits which you have acquired through the dispassion of divine love[2] and thus you have also become rich with the heavenly treasure.[3] "Moreover, the sons do not stock up on treasure for the fathers, but the fathers for the sons."[4] Since you are "fathers," imitate the "father" Christ and feed us with "barley loaves"[5] through the teaching of the improvement of morals. Stoop to our acerbity until we have put off the animalistic morals[6] from ourselves and have become worthy of the spiritual "bread," "that has come down

[1]See the Foreword.
[2]Cf. *Pr* 81.
[3]Cf. Mt 12.35. This heavenly treasure means knowledge (cf. *Ep* 47.1), or wisdom (cf. Wis 7.14).
[4]2 Cor 12.14.
[5]Jn 6.9. These barley loaves here are a symbol of praxis.
[6]Cf. *Sk* 40; *M.c.* 18; *Ep.Mel.* 41.46; *in Eccl* 3.19: Géhin 21.

from heaven"[7] and which nourishes all natures endowed with logos according to the measure of their condition.[8]

But then in another place Evagrius says with regard to spiritual fathers: "It is the fathers' place to educate the sons with regard to virtue and the knowledge of God; to give the children wisdom, however, is the Lord's place."[9] It is a similar case with the holy angels, who "purify us from vice and make us dispassionate through the insights of admonition; they free us from ignorance, however, through the insights of nature and divine ideas (*logoi*), making us wise and knowledgeable."[10]

Finally, if we intend those who "have attained spiritual knowledge," and therefore have themselves become true gnostics, so that they "will help the holy angels to lead rational souls from vice back to virtue and from ignorance back to knowledge,"[11] then it will be clear what kind of fatherhood Christ's is and in what relationship it stands to the "spiritual fatherhood" of the true gnostic.

> Know that God watches over all things through Christ and that he exercises his providence over all things through his holy angels, who are exceedingly rich in knowledge of things on earth.[12] The "helpers" of the holy angels, however, are the "ancient fathers," whom for that very reason we "should honor as the angels."[13]

The heavenly fatherhood of Christ manifests itself among us men in the angel-like service of the spiritual father, through whom Christ operates. For what Paul said about himself is true about the spiritual father in its most ideal form: "I no longer live, but Christ lives in me."[14] "So, all those who resemble the apostle through their conduct, merit

---

[7]Jn 6.38 more commonly. This heavenly bread, which is Christ, symbolizes here the knowledge of Christ, cf. *in Prov* 19.24: Géhin 203 more commonly.

[8]*Ep* 61.1. Cf. *Ep.fid.* 4; *in Prov* 17.2: Géhin 153; idem. 19.17: Géhin 199.

[9]*In Prov* 19.14: Géhin 197.

[10]*KG* 4.35. Cf. *KG* 6.86.

[11]*KG* 6.90. The focus here is on the last sentence of this work, from which it becomes clear toward whom it is primarily directed.

[12]*In Eccl* 5.7–11: Géhin 38.4–6. Cf. 2 Sam 14.20, 36.

[13]*Pr* 100.

[14]Gal 2.20.

being called 'father' by the Holy Spirit, who lives in them." For, "a man who 'begets' another in the work of God, is his father in accordance with God, in this world as much as in the coming one."[15] Concretely, the spiritual "son" experiences this fatherhood of Christ by obediently submitting to the instructions of the father. We wish to deepen these thoughts step by step in what follows.

*

To be a father means—in the literal sense, as much as in the figurative sense that is derived from it—to bestow individual being and life upon another being in the process of begetting. It is in this sense that God the Father is in an absolute sense the "Father of the Son."[16] This being-a-father of God is as much without beginning as it is unrepeatable. God does not become Father; he is Father by very nature of his being,[17] and for this reason the Son is also "consubstantial" with the Father.[18] This Son is thus also his "uniquely begotten,"[19] after whom there is no other.[20]

"Father" and "Son," nevertheless, are terms that express a relationship. In a derivative sense, then, God can also be designated "Father of intelligible beings,"[21] because he is the Origin and "Father of all."[22] Indeed, he is their Creator, and together with Wisdom, our Mother, he "begot"[23] them all; that is to say, he called them into being. He exercises this fatherhood vis-à-vis creatures in Christ.

The devil can also be called "father" in a derivative sense, as Christ himself did;[24] that is, he is called "father" insofar as he "begets"[25] godless

---

[15]L.T. Lefort, *Les Vies coptes de Saint Pachôme et de ses premiers successeurs* (Löwen, 1943), 54f.

[16]*KG* 6.4.

[17]*Ep.Mel.* 25.

[18]*Ep.fid.* 2.8.

[19]Jn 1.14 (only-begotten) more commonly.

[20]*KG* 4.16.

[21]*Ep* 58.3. Cf. *KG* 4.20; *Ep* 57.3.

[22]Eph 4.6. Cf. *in Prov* 30.17: Géhin 294.

[23]*In Prov* 6.20: Géhin 79.

[24]Jn 8.44.

[25]Cf. *in Prov* 6.29: Géhin 83. Concerning the devil as "father," cf. also 17 *in Ps* 9.33; 7 *in Ps* 26.20; 7 *in Ps* 108.9.

sons, with vice serving as the mother; this refers to those who were created originally good and were corrupted through sin. He is even called "god," as in Psalm 95.5, but only mendaciously,[26] since he is that "new god" from Psalm 80.10 who is unable "to bestow being."[27] His "fatherhood," therefore, is also thoroughly relative: it is incapable of begetting ultimately evil beings. Evil has no substance, regardless of how real it might be.

Against this background one can understand in what sense Christ can bear the title "father" (or even "mother"); this happens often[28] in the ancient Christian and early monastic literature, although it has a particular meaning in Evagrian Christology.

> "The torch of him who speaks ill of his father or his mother
> will die out,
> and the pupil of his eyes will see darkness":
>
> Depending on the perspective the one and the same Christ can be designated "father" as well as "mother": he can be designated as the father of those who possess the "spirit of sonship,"[29] but as mother of those who still need milk and not solid nourishment.[30] In this way indeed was the Christ who spoke in Paul[31] the "father" of the Ephesians inasmuch as he revealed[32] to them the mysteries of wisdom, but he was the "mother" of the Corinthians[33] inasmuch as he fed them with milk.[34]

The fact that Evagrius calls Christ not only "father" but also "mother" in this passage makes it clear that even if he did not expressly say

[26]*Ep.fid.* 3.9f.

[27]4 *in Ps* 80.10 = *KG* 5.49.

[28]Cf. B. Steidle, "Heilige Vaterschaft," *Benediktinische Monatsschrift* 14 (1932): 217ff., and "Abba-Vater," *Benediktinische Monatsschrift* 16 (1934): 89–101; G. Racle, "A propos du Christ-Père," *RSR* (1962): 400–408; A. de Vogüé, "La Paternité du Christ dans la Règle de saint Benoît et du Maître," *La Vie spirituelle* 110 (1964): 55–67.

[29]Rom 8.15.

[30]Heb 5.12.

[31]Cf. Gal 2.20; 2 Cor 13.3.

[32]The revelation of the mystery of Christ is one of the central themes of the Epistle to the Ephesians.

[33]1 Cor 3.2.

[34]*In Prov* 20.9a: Géhin 210.

so, these names refer to different aspects (*epinoia*) of Christ. Namely, Christ took on numerous functions appropriate to the necessities of his creatures by reason of the salvific economy; these functions are mirrored in the different names that the Holy Scriptures ascribe to him, e.g., "way,"[35] "door,"[36] "shepherd,"[37] "high priest," "apostle,"[38] etc.[39]

In this sense Christ has also become the teacher[40] of men, insofar as he is also their "father." He turns into wise men those whom he has made worthy[41] of his "friendship" through the revelation of the mysteries of wisdom. Christ is in effect "the only mediator between God and men,"[42] since he is indeed "true God" and "true man" on account of our human nature, which he assumed.

Flesh of Christ:
the practical virtues.
He who eats them,
becomes dispassionate.[43]

Blood of Christ:
Contemplation of created beings,
and he who drinks it
thereby becomes wise.[44]

Chest of the Lord:
Knowledge of God.
He who on it reclines,
becomes a theologian.[45]

---

[35]Jn 14.6.
[36]Jn 10.9.
[37]Jn 10.11.
[38]Heb 3.1.
[39]*Ep.fid.* 8.5.
[40]*KG* 6.20.
[41]Cf. Géhin, P. *Scholies aux Proverbes* 53–54.
[42]1 Tim 2.5.
[43]*Mn* 118.
[44]*Mn* 119.
[45]Mn 120. [The reference is clearly to John the Apostle, who later came to be known as John the Theologian, who was reclining on the Lord's chest when Peter made gestures to him to inquire who would betray Christ after the Last Supper. See Jn 21.20.—*Tr.*]

The role of Christ as "only mediator between God and men" is a reality decisive not only for the understanding of the complete salvific economy of God,[46] but also one that comes to full effect precisely in mysticism as internalized theology, and again as "unceasing prayer."[47] For the "Lord"[48] whom we invoke "with tears"[49] while keeping watch is, in fact, Christ![50]

> Pray
> without ceasing
> and remember Christ,
> who begets you.[51]

This advice is directed to the consecrated virgin Severa, although it naturally applies to every Christian who through the Holy Spirit is "begotten" for eternal life at baptism. It applies in particular to the spiritual father (or spiritual mother) who, as we have already seen, is a coworker of the holy angels, through whom Christ accomplishes his salvific work.

*

If an essential aspect of fatherhood is the imparting of divine wisdom, then it makes sense that spiritual fatherhood is primarily the *imitation* of this fatherhood of Christ, as we saw above.

> "Fathers will distribute house and goods among their children,
> but it is the Lord who unites the wife to her husband in harmony":

> It is the fathers' place to educate the sons with regard to virtue and the knowledge of God; to give the children wisdom, however, is the Lord's place.[52]

Human and divine action are differentiated very finely here: the human spiritual father directs toward virtue and knowledge of

---

[46] *In Eccl* 5.7–11: Géhin 38.
[47] 1 Thess 5.17. Cf. Bunge, *Das Geistgebet*, chapter 2.
[48] *M.c.* 34.18ff. (cf. Ps 139.8 and 30.3).
[49] *Vg* 25.
[50] *Pr* 54.
[51] *Vg* 5.
[52] *In Prov* 19.14: Géhin 197.

God,[53] but the Lord himself gives divine wisdom, that "wife" who was given us from youth,[54] since the gnostic is only a "shield-bearer of wisdom."[55] All the same, the spiritual father does not really "beget" his sons by himself, since that is the role of the "spiritual charism" which was given him, namely, "that which has the ability to beget through virtue and through the knowledge of God."[56]

The following text from the *Sentences for Monks*, which so often talks about "fathers" and "sons," should be understood in the above sense:

> A monk who desists
> from keeping the word of his father
> will dishonor the gray hairs of him
> who begets him,
> and will revile the life of his children,
> but the Lord will scorn him.[57]

"Children" (of the spiritual father) refers here to those whom Evagrius also calls "sons of the sons," since they were made worthy of the same "spirit of sonship,"[58] because those whom Evagrius above named "fathers" were initially themselves "sons"; that is, they were sons of Christ, who is their "father."

> "You should always have a friend,
> and your brothers will be helpful to you in affliction,
> since they were begotten for that purpose":

If the sons of Christ are brothers to one another, but the angels and righteous men are sons of Christ, then the angels and holy men are also brothers to one another, since they were begotten through the same spirit of sonship.[59]

---

[53]Cf. chapter XII below.

[54]*In Prov* 5.18: Géhin 64.

[55]*KG* 5.65. In Greek the term is *hypaspistēs*. One could also translate: man-at-arms, bodyguard, etc.

[56]*Ep* 52.7.

[57]*Mn* 88.

[58]12 *in Ps* 102.18.

[59]*In Prov* 17.17: Géhin 163.

According to Evagrius, who is here following his teacher Gregory of Nazianzus,[60] this "spirit of sonship"[61] means "wisdom,"[62] for, according to Isaiah 11.2 and 1 Corinthians 12.8, it is the first gift of grace of the Holy Spirit.[63] For that reason, Evagrius likewise designates the "spirit of sonship" as a *charisma*.[64] The same "spirit of sonship" is incidentally also the source of "spiritual friendship," about which Evagrius speaks in such delightful words.[65]

*

Thus, no one becomes a "son" of the "Father" of Christ, and thereby a "wise man," unless he becomes a "father" to others. The text cited above goes on:

> They [i.e., the angels and the righteous] were begotten by wisdom for this reason: so that they might lead men from vice to virtue and from ignorance to the knowledge of God, for indeed even[66] "creation itself groans and suffers the pangs of childbirth" and "was unwillingly subjected to vanity."[67]

Spiritual fatherhood is thus not an isolated phenomenon found on its own, but rather for Evagrius it has a very particular theological place in salvation history. It is, as we have already seen, an "imitation" of Christ; that is to say, it is a certain stepping into his salvific work[68] that can lead men from vice to virtue by means of praxis, and from ignorance to knowledge of God, by means of contemplation. It is, therefore, "brotherhood" between the angels and the righteous, since our Redeemer accomplishes his salvific work for us through the former.

It must now be shown what this means more specifically.

---

[60] *Oration* 31.29; cf. 20.6.
[61] Rom 8.15.
[62] *KG* 6.51.
[63] *In Prov* 8.10–11: Géhin 101.
[64] *In Prov* 6.19: Géhin 78.
[65] Cf Géhin, P. *Scholies aux Proverbes*, 53f.
[66] Cf. Rom 8.20–22.
[67] *In Prov* 17.17: Géhin 164.
[68] Cf. *Pr* 1: "Christianity is the teaching of Christ our Redeemer, which consists in those of practice, those of nature, and those of theology." Cf. *Ep.fid.* 4.19ff.

CHAPTER VI

"A Spiritual Grace"

Ironically, Evagrius was accused of never having understood how to integrate Trinitarian theology into his mysticism. For this reason he was also characterized as being more philosophical than theological, given that the three divine persons, but especially the Holy Spirit, supposedly did not play a role worth mentioning in his "ascent of the intellect."[1] This prejudice never wanes, but it too is an anachronism, as we can easily show.[2]

For how could he who so energetically defended the consubstantiality of the Holy Spirit[3] (since the denial of the divinity of the Spirit inevitably takes away from the salvific value of baptism[4]) have misunderstood the role of the Holy Spirit in "spiritual life," as we say today? Of course, we do not yet find in him the abstract concept of "spirituality"; it was likely Jausep Hazzaya who coined it,[5] and he, for his part, was strongly influenced by Evagrius. The Syrian mystic of the eighth century calls the last of the three steps of the spiritual life *ruhanutha*—literally, "spiritualness"—since here the Holy Spirit, who until then was only operating unseen in a man, "personally" steps out into the open and takes the reins.

Upon closer examination, it turns out that in the corresponding writings of the Pontic monk the Spirit is everywhere present and arranges all things. This applies also to the spiritual father, since according to reports of his student, Palladius, Evagrius was himself a "Spirit-bearer

[1]I. Hausherr, *Les leçons d'un contemplativ*, Paris 1960, 98.

[2]Cf. G. Bunge, *Geistgebet*, Chapter VI; also, "L'Esprit compatissant. L'Esprit Saint, Maître de la 'prière véritable' dans la spiritualité d'Évagre le Pontique," *Buisson Ardent* 13 (2007): 106–12.

[3]Cf. *Ep.fid.* 10 and 11.

[4]*In Prov* 22.28: Géhin 249.

[5]Cf. Bunge, *Briefe*, 187ff.

(*pneumatophoros*) full of gifts of discernment" (*diakritikos*).[6] These are
defined in a letter as follows:

> With regard to spiritual fathers, they are certainly not called
> "fathers" by reason of being the superiors of many. Otherwise, one
> could also call the tribunes "fathers." Fathers are, on the contrary,
> those who have the spiritual gift that has the power to beget many
> through virtue and the knowledge of God.[7]

The Holy Spirit is also he who inspired the words of the Scriptures
that the gnostic has to interpret[8] and which, for that very reason, are
"spiritual words."[9] The Holy Spirit is he who speaks[10] through these
words that are full of "spiritual instruction."[11] The Holy Spirit is he who
reveals[12] the knowledge of the mysteries to the gnostic (or contemplative). For this reason, this suprarational knowledge (or contemplation)
is also consistently designated as "spiritual."

Furthermore, not only is the Holy Spirit the one whose gift of grace
effects that one becomes a "spiritual father," he is also the one who
brings about the "spiritual teacher,"[13] "spiritual direction,"[14] "spiritual
friendship"[15] and with it the "spiritual brother,"[16] "spiritual virtues,"[17]
"spiritual love,"[18] "spiritual joy."[19] In brief, he is the one who brings
about all those "fruits of the Spirit,"[20] through which the Holy Spirit,
whom Christ received through the "spiritual seal"[21] of baptism, comes

---

[6] *HL* 11: Butler 34.11.
[7] Ep 52.7 (Greek fragment).
[8] Cf. *Gn* 18.34.
[9] *M.c.* 23 at the end; *Mn* 47.
[10] *M.c.* 18.37; *Ep* 56.3.
[11] 5 *in Ps* 28.7; *in Prov* 22.10: Géhin 240.
[12] 59 *in Ps* 118.131; *KG* 2.59; 3.77; 6.44.
[13] *Or* 139.
[14] *M.c.* 20.7.
[15] *In Prov* 6.1: Géhin 69.
[16] *Or* 109.
[17] *Or* 132.
[18] *Or* 77; *Pr* 35; *KG* 3.58.
[19] *Eul* 6; cf. *Or* 143; *in Eccl* 2.10: Géhin 9; idem 3.19–2: Géhin 21.
[20] 18 *in Ps* 87.13.
[21] *Mn* 124; cf. *Ep.fid.* 10.12f.

to be manifest[22] in our life in many ways, culminating in "spiritual prayer," the prayer "in spirit and truth"—that is to say, prayer in the Holy Spirit and in the only-begotten Son, whose crowning it is.[23]

Only thanks to the omnipresence of the Holy Spirit can we rightly speak, as we do today, about a "spiritual life." In that "spiritual prayer," the mystic receives already here on earth a foretaste of the eschatological bliss in which we will participate (once we have been united eternally with the Spirit and the Son) when we attain unmediated access to the Father[24] through these "mediators" who alone are eternal, since they are uncreated.

So, there can be absolutely no talk about Evagrius never having understood how to integrate Trinitarian theology into his mysticism, which is supposedly characterized as more philosophical than theological, and in which the Holy Spirit especially did not play a role worthy of mention. "As the question, so the answer." Anyone who regards Evagrius primarily as a philosopher and interprets him accordingly, while failing to take into account the fact that he regards the Holy Scriptures as the only safe source of inspiration for theology,[25] will never understand the Pontic monk.

*

Whenever Evagrius uses the adjective "spiritual," we can be sure that he never does it without direct relationship to the Third Person of the Holy Trinity. Words in Evagrius still have their natural weight and are not, as in modern colloquial speech, used purely habitually. This is why his gnostic is a "wise" man, because he himself was "begotten" by Wisdom;[26] he is "spiritual" because he has received a "spiritual gift"; he is "father" because this charism "begets" many *through* him for virtue and the knowledge of God.

This "gift" is not, at any rate, something simply external. Instead, it transforms from within the one gifted. For the gnostic becomes

---

[22]*Ep* 18.3; 30.1; 58.3.
[23]Cf. Bunge, *Geistgebet*, chapter VI.
[24]*Ep.Mel.* 31.
[25]Cf. *Ep.fid.* 2.4–6!
[26]*In Prov* 17.17: Géhin 164.

"spiritual" by "cleaving to the Lord";[27] that is to say, by cleaving to the Holy Spirit[28] (according to the Evagrian exegesis of 2 Corinthians 3.17), who is also "Lord" (the Creed), and with whom he becomes "a spirit."[29] In other words, the gnostic becomes "spiritual" through participation in the Holy Spirit.

> "The streams clap their hands in unison": When the Holy Spirit's gifts of grace are called "streams" (based on the verse: "Streams of living water will flow out of his body),"[30] then also those who partake of these "streams" will themselves suitably be called "streams"....[31]

Palladius, who as a perennial student and confidant of Evagrius was wholly steeped in the spirit of the master, does not shy away from applying the Pauline designation "spiritually gifted" (*pneumatikos*) to those "fathers" *and* "mothers"—take note—who had received this spiritual charism. Abba as much as Amma are in effect, as he expressly establishes, the conventional titles for these spiritually gifted people.[32] As mentioned above, his own teacher Abba Evagrius[33] was expressly a "Spirit-bearer" for him. By saying this, he placed him on the same level as the greats of his time,[34] such as Abba John of Lykopolis, whom Evagrius himself honored highly and whom he once sought out in person.[35]

*

The only way, then, that leads to the attainment of this ontologically unattainable charism is praxis, that "spiritual method that purifies the

---

[27] *Or* 6.17.

[28] 5 *in Ps* 15.9.

[29] 3 *in Ps* 62.9.

[30] Jn 7.38.

[31] 4 *in Ps* 97.8.

[32] *HL* 34: Butler 99, 18.

[33] He rejected it about himself out of modesty. Cf. 11 *in Ps* 67.15 and *Ep* 58.5, where Evagrius expressed his regret that he himself was not a "stream (of grace) of the Lord."

[34] *HL* 11: Butler 34, 11. In the *Apophthegmata*, Antonius (*Antonius* 30) and Macarius the Great (*Macarius* 38) bear this title of honor.

[35] *HL* 35: Butler 103, 2. For the whole, cf. Draguet, R. "L'Histoire Lausiaque,' une oeuvre écrite dans l'esprit d'Évagre," *RHE* 41 (1946), 321ff. under number 177.

passionate part of the soul."[36] In it, man becomes suited through personal dedication to that which was freely given to him in baptism.

"I opened my mouth and inhaled the Spirit": He who through praxis opens[37] his "heart"[38] inhales the Holy Spirit, who reveals[39] to him the mysteries of God.[40]

He who steps into the realm of knowledge becomes a gnostic, someone "graced with knowledge." He, then, enters the kingdom of the Holy Spirit, who is also always the Spirit of Christ. The gnostic who "reclined on the chest of the Lord" in order to obtain knowledge of God becomes, by virtue of such an intimate familiarity (which man can only receive),[41] a "theologian"[42] in the true meaning of the word. For his wisdom is no longer the "external"[43] type of this world; his knowledge is no longer that "gloomy" type, accessible to the demons themselves;[44] nor, especially, is it the fruit of either zealous study[45] or dialectical sharpness, which one finds also among the impure.[46] It derives, rather, from divine grace;[47] it is first and foremost the Holy Spirit's gift of grace.[48]

> He who loves honey,[49]
> will eat his honeycomb,
> and he who gathers it,
> will be filled with the Spirit.[50]

[36]*Pr* 78.

[37]On this "opening" cf. *in Prov* 20.12: Géhin 216.

[38]The symbolism is to be resolved as follows: Mouth = heart (2 *in Ps* 140.3), heart = intellect (4 *in Ps* 15.9 etc.).

[39]59 *in Ps* 118.31.

[40]1 Cor 2.10.

[41]*Ep.Mel.* 67.

[42]*Mn* 120; cf. *Or* 61.

[43]*Gn* 4.

[44]*KG* 6.2.

[45]*Gn* 45.

[46]*Ep* 62.1–3, cf. *KG* 4.90.

[47]*Gn* 4.45 more commonly.

[48]*In Prov* 8.10: Géhin 101.

[49]Honey is the symbol of knowledge: *KG* 3.64; cf. 3.67 (Ps 18.10); 7 *in Ps* 80.17; 45 *in Ps* 118.103; *in Prov* 6.8: Géhin 72; idem 24.13: Géhin 270.

[50]*Mn* 115.

CHAPTER VII

The Spiritual Father
as True "Gnostic"

Thanks to the spiritual charism given to him by God, the most important task of the spiritual father is "to beget many for virtue and the knowledge of God," of which he himself has become a participant. In fact, the spiritual father is a "gnostic." Evagrius does not shy away from using this name, which at that time was significantly less charged than it is today. In doing so he joins Clement of Alexandria,[1] who in his contests with that "falsely so-called gnosis" likewise was not about to sacrifice the ideal of a "true gnosis" and of the gnostic to its falsifications.

The Evagrian gnostic is a "just man" and a "holy man"[2] to the degree that he becomes "knowledgeable" and "wise," since before he becomes a *theōrētikos* himself (a beholder or contemplative) he himself has already travelled on the road of praxis. This alone makes him "worthy of knowledge": "He who has anchored himself firmly in the virtues and has mixed himself entirely with them, he, I say, thinks no more of the law, or the commandments, or the punishments, but rather he says and does that which his noble disposition tells him."[3]

In fact, when he was come to perfection, the Christian is "no longer under the law, but under grace,"[4] and "perfect love drives all fear from him."[5] He has come to *apatheia*, that natural (i.e., given at creation)

---

[1]Cf. Guillaumont, "Le gnostique chez Clément d'Alexandrie et chez Évagre le Pontique," *Études sur la spiritualité de l'Orient Chrétien*, Spiritualité Orientale 66, Bellefontaine (1996): 151–160.

[2]*In Prov* 17.17: Géhin 163, more commonly.

[3]*Pr* 70.

[4]Rom 6.14.

[5]1 Jn 4.18.

"health of the soul,"[6] and this "noble disposition," the full bloom sown in created nature and renewed through baptism,[7] the indelible "seeds of virtue"[8] tell him what he should do or speak.

This lofty ideal, described in detail in the book of the *Gnostikos*, does not, however, blind Evagrius to reality! Moreover, he forcibly admonishes the gnostic, like Paul, to keep his body, the locus of the lower passions, disciplined.[9] Freedom from the law never means libertinism; rather, it means only the uncompelled and the "natural" doing of the good. The state of the gnostic is also not an inalienable possession; Evagrius knows not only a certain "temptation of the gnostic,"[10] but also a certain "sin of the gnostic."[11] By way of warning, Evagrius says: "A harsh accuser of the gnostic is his conscience, and it is impossible to hide anything from it, for it 'recognizes the hidden things of the heart.'"[12]

The following does not attempt to trace in every detail the picture of the gnostic as Evagrius outlines it in the fifty chapters dedicated to him in the book.[13] It must suffice us here to underline those characteristics by virtue of which we can most clearly differentiate the true gnostic from the false gnostic.

All the virtues direct the gnostic on the way (of knowledge), but above all freedom from anger. Namely, he who has touched upon knowledge and is easily moved by anger is like him who gouges out his own eyes with an iron needle.[14]

If the "door of knowledge" is meek love, which makes the intellect "contemplative" (*theōrētikos*), then anger[15] as its adversary indeed blinds it. Thus, the temptation to anger—particularly in its solidified form,

---

[6]*Pr* 56.
[7]Cf. Bunge, *Geistgebet*, chapter IV.
[8]*Ep* 18.2; 43.3, more commonly.
[9]Gn 37 (cf. *Or* 9.27).
[10]*Gn* 42.
[11]*Gn* 43.
[12]*Gn* 39, cf. Ps 43.22.
[13]On that, cf. the introduction of the editor of that work.
[14]Gn 5.
[15]*KG* V.27.

rancor—mainly afflicts the "seasoned,"[16] who, owing to their long asceticism, should in reality have become "contemplatives." Evagrius tirelessly denounces the disastrous consequences of anger.[17]

If we read Church history from this perspective, then many dark periods appear in a different light. For, as Evagrius (among other fathers) teaches, heresies are ultimately the work of demons,[18] but the demon is essentially anger.[19] Many dogmatic controversies would certainly have gone otherwise if those engaged in them had been aware that he who allows himself to be ruled by anger gouges out that "right and left" eye of the intellect, by which we are able contemplatively to know God and his creation.[20]

The primordial virtue of the gnostic, then, is angerlessness or, put affirmatively, meekness, which is the concrete manifestation of love.[21] This meekness, often opposed to arrogance,[22] is, as we saw, an aristocratic virtue par excellence. For the Holy Scriptures speak only of Christ and his Old Testament prefigurations, Moses and David, as "meek." It is the virtue of the just man, who is up to the task of dedicating himself to the other; he can also be the greatest sinner, like the people of Israel who apostatized from God in the desert. Evagrius dedicated the most beautiful pages of his personal letters to this feat of Moses, whom he represents with predilection as the ideal of meekness.

The first[23] and original[24] commandment is love, with which the intellect sees original love,[25] namely, God.[26] Through our love we see the love of God for us,[27] as is written in the Psalm: "He will

---

[16]*Gn* 31, cf. *Pr* 63.

[17]*Or* 48.51; *M.c.* 5, 9, 16, 23, 27; *Mn* 34.112; *Vg* 8, 19, 41, 45; *Ep* 4.2, 4.5; 6.4; 11.3; 15 etc.

[18]*Ep.fid.* 2.6ff. (The "Philistines" symbolize demons, cf. *KG* 5.30). Cf. also 1 *in Ps* 141.4; *KG* 1.10 and the biographical text *Vita* O, which has its counterpart in *Mn* 126.

[19]*KG* 1.68; 3.34; 4.47; 9 *in Ps* 73.19.

[20]*M.c.* 42.

[21]Cf. Bunge, *Briefe*, 126ff.

[22]*In Prov* 17.9: Géhin 176.

[23]Mt 12.29ff.

[24]1 Jn 2.7 etc.

[25]Cf. for the expression also *Ant* 1.64.

[26]1 Jn 4.8.

[27]Cf. 1 *in Ps* 17.2: Since like is known by like, we recognize love through love.

teach the meek his ways."[28] "Moses, however, was meeker than all men,"[29] and the Holy Spirit appropriately says: "He showed Moses his ways."[30]

Teach this meekness to your brothers to spare them remorse at their anger. For no evil turns the intellect into a demon as much as anger in the confusion of rage.[31] The Psalm says: "Your anger is like that of the serpent."[32] And we should [also] not think that the demon is nothing but a human who is incensed by anger and deprived of his perception! For the bodies of demons have color and form, but they elude our perception, since their quality is not similar to the quality of the bodies subject to our sensory perception. Therefore, they imitate our bodies in many ways when they want to appear to someone and do not show their own bodies.

Therefore, let no brother become similar to the serpent; condone no abstinence among you that is far from meekness. For he who abstains from food and drink but because of this motivates irrational anger, is like a boat in the middle of the sea that has a demon of anger for a steersman.

But tell me, why did the Scriptures, as they praised Moses, leave aside all wondrous signs and solely recollect meekness? For they do not say that Moses chastened Egypt with the twelve plagues, or that he led the chosen people out of it. And they do not say that Moses was the first to receive the law from God or that he caught a glimpse of the appearance of bygone worlds. And they do not say that he parted the Sea of Reeds with his rod or made water to gush out of the rock for the thirsty people. Rather, they say that he, all alone in the desert, stood before the face of God even as he wanted to annihilate Israel, and asked to be wiped out with the sons of his people.[33] He set before God love of mankind

[28]Ps 24.9.

[29]Num 12.3.

[30]Ps 102.7.

[31]Cf. G. Bunge, *Drachenwein und Engelsbrot: Die Lehre des Evagrios Pontikos von Zorn und Sanftmut* (Würzburg, 1999).

[32]Ps 57.5, cf. 25 *in Ps* 17.49.

[33]Cf. 11 *in Ps* 105.23: "It is noteworthy that a single holy man, like Moses, was in the position to deflect the anger of God, weighing on the whole people."

and transgression by saying: "Forgive them or blot me out of the book you have written."[34] Thus spoke the meek one! But God preferred to forgive them who had sinned than to commit an injustice against Moses.

The Scriptures pass over the famed feeding with the manna and the unexpected flock of quail, and Moses' fasting that went beyond human nature, and also the allegorical tabernacle, in which the bygone and future worlds were represented,[35] and they praise alone this, that "Moses was meeker than all men."

What a wonder! Indeed [the Scriptures] captured the wisdom of the man in two syllables! For the lavish praise of Moses, just like his name, consists in two syllables.[36]

Mindful of this virtue, David also called upon God by saying: "Remember, Lord, David and all his meekness."[37] Not that his knees became weak from fasting and that his flesh [for want] of oil was fading,[38] or that he kept the night watch and became like a sparrow who flies around roofs,[39] but rather: "Remember, O Lord, David and all his meekness."

So, let us also imitate this meekness, by which he who says, "Learn from me, for I am meek and humble of heart,"[40] might teach us his ways and save us.[41]

After this praise, one understands why Evagrius can say that no virtue can make the intellect as receptive to knowledge as meekness. "Abstinence oppresses the body alone; meekness, however, makes the intellect a beholder (i.e., contemplative)."[42]

The highest praise that Evagrius can lavish on a trusted friend (Rufinus?) can therefore be nothing other than:

[34]Ex 32.32.
[35]Cf. Heb 9:6ff.
[36]In Greek, the words "meek" (*praos*) and "Moses" both consist of two syllables.
[37]Ps 131.1.
[38]Ps 108.24.
[39]Ps 101.8.
[40]Mt 11.29.
[41]Ep 56.3–9. Our translation follows as far as possible the Greek fragment of the letter, as far as it is preserved.
[42]*Ep* 27.4; cf. *Ep* 33.2; 34.2.

I am indeed convinced that your meekness has become a cause for greater knowledge. For no single virtue brings about wisdom as much as meekness, for the sake of which Moses was also praised as having been "meeker than all men." And I, too, pray to become and be called a student of the "meek."[43]

Nor does Evagrius tire of explaining[44] the meaning of meekness, for which some biblical passages regularly serve him as cases in point.[45] This anchoring in revelation teaches once more that the Evagrian ideal has its firm locus in theology, and for that reason can only be understood and lived out on that basis.

*

Meekness, that "true crown of white hairs of the aged,"[46] manifests itself concretely in many ways. The spiritual father of Evagrius is "merciful"[47] and "selfless";[48] he would rather suffer injustice than to seek his perhaps justified right in the process.[49] In his behavior with others he is neither inaccessible nor morose. It is the part of the former not to know the meaning of the things that happen (through God); of the latter, like the demon,[50] "not to will that all men be saved and that they may come to the knowledge of God."[51]

In his external behavior itself, then, the spiritual father reflects the insight into the hidden salvific will of the Father that was granted him, his "unfathomable love"[52] that in a single sweep loves everything it created, infinitely transcending the common, selfish human understanding.

[43]*Ep* 36.2.

[44]*Ep* 19.2; 27.2; 33.2; 34.2; 59.2; 3 *in Ps* 24.4; 4 *in Ps* 44.5; 1 *in Ps* 131.1; *Or* 14; *Pr* 20; *M.c.* 23; 27; *Sk* 3.

[45]These are above all three Scriptural passages: Num 12.3 (cf. above, note 42), Joel 3.11 (*Ep* 16.6; 24.2; *Eul* 11), and of course Mt 11.29 (*Ep* 36.3; 56.9; *M.c.* 13).

[46]*Mn* 111.

[47]*Gn* 7.

[48]*Gn* 24.

[49]*Gn* 8, cf. *Ep* 33.1.

[50]15 *in Ps* 67.24.

[51]*Gn* 22 (cf. 1 Tim 2.4).

[52]*Ep.Mel.* 14.

Although in his being the gnostic is accessible, kind, and of a meek love, he will not wonder at being the object of slander, whether from men,[53] as Evagrius himself experienced,[54] or from demons.[55] Rather, he will endure all temptations steadfastly,[56] abstain from all manner of wrangling,[57] and respond to slander with silence, rather than with contradiction.[58]

We could mistake this picture of the spiritual father for a simple idealization removed from reality, did we not know that Evagrius himself openly represented it, as did other monks, friends, and contemporaries such as Macarius the Great, Pambo, Ammonius, and those of steadfast character whom he extols in his treatise *On Prayer*.[59] Such a lofty ideal becomes all the more a reality when it is borne out as true and worthy of realization.

[53] *Gn* 32.
[54] *Ep* 51.2; 52.4f.; 59.2.
[55] *KG* 3.90.
[56] *Gn* 46.
[57] *Ep* 52.5.
[58] *Ep* 52.7.
[59] *Or* 106–109; 111–112.

CHAPTER VIII

Physician and Teacher

A ccording to the two steps of the spiritual life, the task of the spiritual father is twofold: "to lead" others "from vice to virtue" on the way of praxis, the exercise of the gospel commandments, and thereafter, through his spiritual guidance, "from ignorance to the knowledge of God." The latter is impossible without the former. The one "ailing" with the "passions" of the soul must first be led to the natural "health of the soul" before his soul can move *logikōs*, freely in line with its natural purpose, and undertake the search for God.[1]

So, the spiritual father is both physician and teacher in one according to the example of Christ, whom Evagrius designates as the "physician of souls" with some predilection, since he, like none other, "knows which medicines lead from vice to virtue and from ignorance to knowledge."[2] Since spiritual fatherhood is imitation of the "Father," Christ, who, for his part, operates in this world through his angels,[3] Evagrius can write: "We should honor our forebears as the angels, for they are those who anoint us for battles and heal the bites of the wild beasts."[4]

Just as the trainers of old anointed athletes with oil for competition in order to make it hard for their opponents to grab hold on them, so also the fathers of old prepared their spiritual students for battle with the demons,[5] whom they likened to the wild beasts, by anointing them with "oil," which is also the symbol of knowledge.[6] By this we should

---

[1]Cf. *Or* 51.
[2]*Ep* 42.2; 51.2; 52.4; 55.3; 57.3; *Ep.fid.* 5.15ff.; *Ep.Mel.* 24.
[3]*In Eccl* 5.7–11: Géhin 38.
[4]*Pr* 100.
[5]9 *in Ps* 73.19; 1 *in Ps* 78.2 = *KG* 1.53.
[6]7 *in Ps* 44.8; 10 *in Ps* 88.21.

understand the salvific teachings of the master, which make it possible for the students to fight with knowledge, not dealing blows blindly "as in the night" (of ignorance).[7] For "the actions of the commandments do not suffice (in and of themselves) fully to heal the capacities of the soul if the corresponding contemplations do not follow in the intellect."[8]

So, it is necessary to undertake praxis "with knowledge."[9] Besides our own meticulous observation,[10] we also need an experienced spiritual father.

*

If the combatant should, nevertheless, be bitten by the "wild beasts," the teacher becomes a physician, and in the place of Christ he administers the appropriate medicine to his students. The "remedies" that this "physician of souls" gives are generally the exercises of practical asceticism: "hunger, thirst, wakefulness, distancing (oneself) from the inhabited world, and prayer";[11] through these coveting and anger are purified and healed.[12] Occasionally Christ, the physician of souls, avails himself of stronger means, such as humiliations and affronts of all sorts,[13] as Evagrius himself suffered at the hands of the fathers in his area.[14]

The spiritual father is, then, in the best sense of the word, a pedagogue, and frequently also a strict educator of his spiritual sons, who himself does not shy away from well-aimed blows.[15] "A good father raises (and chastens) his sons; a bad father will direct them to corruption."[16]

The "healing of the bites of the wild beasts" can thus be very painful for those affected by them, since the ancient physicians used the *kauter*,

[7]*Pr* 83.
[8]*Pr* 79.
[9]*Pr* 50.
[10]*Pr* 51 more commonly.
[11]*Ep* 55.3.
[12]*Gn* 47; *Pr* 54.
[13]*Ep* 51.2; 52.4.
[14]Apophthegma *Evagrius* 7. Cf. Bunge, *Briefe*, 81f.
[15]Cf. Heb 12.6ff. "Whom the Lord loves, him he chastens" (Prov 3.12). In Greek *paideuein* means "raise" as much as "chasten," since the former accompanies the later.
[16]*Mn* 2. Cf. *in Prov* 2.2: Géhin 3.

the surgical burning iron, for infected wounds:[17] "The gnostic has the effect of salt for the impure. . . ."[18]

Evagrius demonstrates yet again his fine gift of psychological observation when he notes that the physician's activity of healing also has an effect on the physician: "He who heals men for the Lord's sake, imperceptibly also heals himself. That is, the remedy the gnostic applies to his neighbor heals the latter as much as possible, but necessarily also heals the former."[19]

*

The comparison between the fathers of old and angels made by Evagrius above is reminiscent of a text we just cited. There Evagrius described the work of the angels and of the saints or righteous (both of whom are "brothers" to each other, since both are "sons of Christ") with the following words: "For, they were begotten by Wisdom for the purpose of leading men from vice to virtue and from ignorance to the knowledge of God."[20]

In fact, Evagrius describes the task of angels in the salvific plan of God as follows:

> Through the insights of admonition the holy angels purify us from vice and make us dispassionate. Through the insights of nature and divine words, however, they free us from ignorance and make us wise men and gnostics.[21]

One can readily recognize the three basic elements in which "Christianity" consists, according to Evagrius: the practical, the natural, and the theological.[22] The angels, therefore, help us to become "Christians" in the full sense of the word! And in this, the true gnostic is instrumental to them: "Whoever has been made worthy of spiritual

---

[17] *Ep* 55.1; *in Prov* 29.1: Géhin 356.
[18] *Gn* 3. Salt is used for the scouring and preservation of foods.
[19] *Gn* 33. Cf. Jsa 5:20.
[20] *In Prov* 17.17: Géhin 164.
[21] *KG* 6.35. Cf. *KG* 6.86.
[22] *Pr* 1.

knowledge will help the holy angels to return rational souls from vice to virtue and from ignorance to knowledge."[23]

The spiritual father takes part in the life of the individual in the role that belongs to the angel "given" to everyone "from youth on"[24]— the personal guardian angel. Evagrius can corroborate this ancient notion of a personal guardian angel not only with Old Testament examples (Saul, Jacob, Zechariah), but also with Christ's saying that "the angels" of these little ones ". . . see the countenance of my Father in heaven all the time."[25] The angel-like activity of the true gnostic is not, incidentally, constrained to this age, but continues also in the "age to come."[26]

*

Not only does teaching belong to the angelic service of the spiritual father, but also intercessory prayer that characterizes the righteous. "It is right to pray not only for one's own purification, but also for that of anyone congeneric,[27] and thus to imitate the angelic beings."[28]

Evagrius plays here with those Scriptural texts that portray the angels round about God as mediators of human prayers.[29] Besides the angels, such mediators also include the saints and the righteous. "A 'supplicatory prayer' is a petition on behalf of someone else, which is presented to God by someone better for the salvation of another."[30]

*

This petition "on behalf of," which furthermore does not preclude sinners,[31] is primordially the duty of the *priest*. Thus it is said of Christ,

---

[23]*KG* 6.90.

[24]*In Prov* 19.4: Géhin 189; cf. *KG* 3.65.

[25]Cf. Mt 18.10. Evagrius cites this verse specifically in the scholia on the Psalter, as evidence that this "seeing the countenance of the Father" reserved for the angels is also possible for humans.

[26]Cf. *KG* 6.24; *Ep* 23; 36.2; 37.3; *In Prov* 28.22: Géhin 354.

[27]*Ep* 53.2: "I call congeneric not only those who are close to us through nature, but those who are so through their condition."

[28]*Or* 40.

[29]Cf. Zech 1.12; Tob 12.12; 15; Rev 8.3f. (cf. *Or* 76).

[30]Sk 30. Evagrius is here interpreting 1 Timothy 2.1.

[31]Cf. 2 *in Ps* 108.4; 7 *in Ps* 108.9; *in Prov* 24.17f.: Géhin 272.

following the Epistle to the Hebrews: "The 'high priest' is he who makes intercession before God for all of rational nature, and who separates some from vice and others from ignorance."[32]

We should remember that "high priest" is one of those aspects and roles that Christ took on for our salvation. Accordingly, since the priest deals *in persona Christi*, Evagrius offers the suggestion: "One should love priests next after the Lord, since they purify us through the holy mysteries and pray for us."[33]

As the context shows, Evagrius is here mainly thinking about priests in the real meaning of the word, such as Macarius the Alexandrian, the priest of Kellia. But he may also have in mind a spiritual meaning of the priesthood, which he unfolds in a letter:

> Praised be God, who entrusted you with the sacred priesthood in order to "baptize" souls in virtue and the knowledge of God.[34] This, indeed, is in truth spiritual priesthood: to receive spiritual knowledge and to call souls from vice to virtue and from ignorance to the "knowledge of Christ." For one intellect is not temporally "older" than (another) intellect. Indeed, what is bodiless is also timeless. He becomes "a priest," rather, when he distinguishes himself in virtue and knowledge.[35]

This scarcely translatable play on words (the term *presbyteros* means "oldest," and a "presbyter" is a priest) becomes understandable when we consider that the spiritual father is also an "elder" (*gerōn*). In another letter, Evagrius adds:

> You have a "treasure"[36] and do not feed us, but rather, you have concealed your "pitcher"[37] from us. And tell us, what should we think about what is written: "Wisdom is a spirit that loves mankind"?[38]

---

[32] *KG* 5.46.
[33] *Pr* 100.
[34] "Baptize" in the literal as well as in the symbolic sense of "plunge in," i.e., fully initiate.
[35] *Ep* 49.1.
[36] Cf. Wis 7.14 (regarding Wisdom); 2 Cor 4.6f.
[37] Cf. 2 *KG* 17.7ff.
[38] Wis 1.6.

Or how does that square with what is said in the Psalm: "The whole day long the righteous is merciful and lends"?[39]

As far as I am concerned, I know that the knowledge of God, by feeding, is fed, and when it gives, it receives! "So break bread for the hungry and lead the homeless into your house."[40] He (that is, the one who gave you the gift of priesthood) asks you to do this with your whole soul![41]

*

In the quoted texts, there is mention again and again of the task that falls to the gnostic "to lead" others "from ignorance to the knowledge of God." So then he is not supposed to keep the "treasure" or "bread," i.e., the knowledge given him, for himself, but is supposed to "feed" the "hungry" through his teaching. The spiritual father of Evagrius is, in the primordial meaning of the word, a "spiritual teacher," "a light for the pure,"[42] since he "illumines"[43] through knowledge those purified by the fire of asceticism.

> You "heirs of God,"
> hear the words[44] of God,
> "Co-heirs of Christ,"[45]
> accept the words of Christ,
> to give them to the hearts of your children
> and to teach them the words of the wise.[46]

He who has become an "heir" of the knowledge of God[47] for the sake of his purity, and has attained deep insight into the mysteries

[39]Ps 36.26.

[40]Is 58.7. "Bread" is here the symbol of knowledge, cf. 3 *in Ps* 23.6; 21 *in Ps* 36.25 more commonly.

[41]*Ep* 47.1–2. Cf. also the commentary by Bunge, *Briefe*, 365f.

[42]*Gn* 3.

[43]Cf. 48 *in Ps* 118.130 more commonly.

[44]These *logoi* are not only the words of the Scriptures, but also and foremost the "ideas" as much of creation as those of *theologia*.

[45]Rom 8.17, cf. *KG* 3.72; 4.8.

[46]*Mn* 1.

[47]Cf. 3 *in Ps* 2.8 more commonly.

of the Scriptures[48] and the salvific operation of God, is called to function as "steward of the mysteries of God,"[49] to which the Scriptures and salvation history bear witness, and to distribute to each one the "nourishment," i.e., knowledge, which his spiritual capacity entails.[50] The following scholion shows how rich this teaching is in blessings:

> "Planted in the house of the Lord, they will sprout blossoms in the courtyard of our God": Planted in the knowledge of the Lord, the righteous will bring many men—in the world as much as in the Church—to blossom, and by their spiritual teaching they will make them bring forth fruits.[51]

*

Incidentally, this teaching consists not only in the positive exposition of truth, but also in the refutation of error that threatens it.

> "He who augments his wealth through interest and usury, gathers it for him who has mercy on the poor": If the "wealth" of the godless is vice, but wise men annihilate it, then the righteous and wise manifestly annihilate vice, by leading the impure to virtue through spiritual teaching.[52]

> "The wise has taken the fortified cities, and razed the citadels in which the godless trusted": Wisdom is a fortified city wherein the wise dwell, who "overthrow [all] thoughts along with every obstacle that exalts itself against the knowledge of Christ."[53]

Nevertheless, the true gnostic does not avail himself of "dialectic"[54] and its verbal disputes, through which he would only be dragged to the side of the false teachers; rather he operates by means of true

---

[48] *Gn* 18.34.
[49] Cf. 1 Cor 4.1.
[50] *In Prov* 17.2: Géhin 153.
[51] 8 *in Ps* 91.14.
[52] *In Prov* 28.8: Géhin 345.
[53] *In Prov* 21.22: Géhin: 229 (cf. 2 Cor 10.5f.).
[54] Cf. *KG* 4.90.

teachings[55] that the demons attempt to ensnare[56] in many ways through heresies in order to cause spiritual "shipwrecks."

"One conducts war with leadership": Those who "suffer shipwreck in regard to the faith"[57] combat the spirits to which theology is opposed, [but] not "with leadership." The same came be said, however, about every virtue. There is, namely, a shipwreck in prudence, love, and freedom from the love of money. And with regard to every one of the teachings of the catholic and apostolic Church, a shipwreck can come about in the same way. But if one must combat the adversary "with leadership," then our life on earth is like a battle at sea.[58]

This charge of teaching is for the gnostic a serious and holy obligation, as one of the letters of admonition to a friend charged with "spiritual priesthood," cited immediately above, taught.

"Free them who are being led to death, and ransom those appointed for slaughter. Do not save yourself!": One should avail oneself of this saying against those who were made worthy of knowledge and neglect the doctrine, while many are led through evil to death (of sins).[59]

"The whole day long the righteous has mercy and lends, and his progeny will be a blessing": He who "lends" words that purify the soul will be blessed, but he who does not pass them on will be cursed.[60]

But woe to them also who lack the tact necessary for the task.

[55]2 *in Ps* 26.3; 2 *in Ps* 29.1; cf. *Ep.fid.* 10.2ff.
[56]1 *in Ps* 141.4.
[57]1 Tim 1.19.
[58]*In Prov* 24.6: Géhin 266.
[59]*In Prov* 24.11: Géhin 269.
[60]22 *in Ps* 36.26.

CHAPTER IX

Spiritual Discretion

I f the guidance of others—that is, their "direction to the knowledge of God" and, for the gnostic, also the fulfillment of a divine obligation—is to take place, it must nevertheless occur with the greatest discretion. The teaching must be guided in its content by the measure of the spiritual capacity of the student. We may not commit everything to anyone and everyone at an arbitrary time. Evagrius is particularly strict on this point and rightly insists that we should not make "books like these" (i.e., mainly the *Kephalaia Gnostika*) accessible to the immature.[1]

Here we are touching on the delicate problem of what is frequently called Evagrian "esotericism." In my opinion, we should speak rather of pedagogical arcane discipline; in a later chapter we will delve into this question extensively.[2] Here the preceding assessment may suffice to show that such a scaled initiation into the mysteries of revelation was most common in ancient Christianity, since it can be found in the case of Christ himself and of Paul, on whom Evagrius leans most often.

*

So, one may not commit everything to anyone and everyone at an arbitrary time. The modern reader often assesses this restraint as merely the sign of a calculating precaution, but according to Gregory of Nazianzus, whom Evagrius invokes as a witness here, it is rather about an essential characteristic of the virtue of justice. "The task of justice is to distribute the meanings (*logoi*) in proportion to the worthiness[3] of

---

[1]*Gn* 25. In letters 600–607 of the two recluses Barsanuphios and John of Gaza, we can infer what error the *Kephalaia Gnostika* of Evagrius would instigate in the head of a young monk.

[2]See below, chapters XI and XII.

[3]One must "have been found worthy" of knowledge, as Evagrius constantly repeats.

each, by which it gives something obscure to note to some, or it suggests something else through riddles, but also clearly says something else for the use of the simple."[4]

Evagrius did this also, as he clearly establishes in his trilogy of the *Praktikos, Gnostikos,* and *Kephalaia Gnostika,*[5] a fact too seldom considered in modern interpretations of his teaching. It simply runs counter to the scientifically oriented mind to grant that there are things that will elude the grasp of analytical understanding, unless one steps into the footsteps of the fathers[6] and takes the toils of praxis upon oneself.

The discretion demanded by justice must be guided by the *worthiness* or, as it is also called, the "condition" or spiritual "state" (*katastasis*) of the hearer, as did Paul, on whom Evagrius calls here.

> "A clever house servant will rule over dimwitted lords and divide the portions among the brothers": If "everyone who does sin is the slave of sin,"[7] then everyone who has kept away from vice and rules over the demons through the virtues "rules the foolish lord."[8] This person will also become a "steward of the mysteries of God"[9] who distributes spiritual knowledge to each of the brothers in proportion to his condition by giving the "Corinthian" "milk" to drink[10] but feeding the "Ephesian" with "solid nourishment"[11] and speaking[12] with him about "height, breadth, length, and depth."[13]

The "measurements" detailed at the end pertain to that "higher teaching concerning the judgment" (of God), which one should conceal before young people and worldly people. "For they do not comprehend the anguish of a rational soul sentenced to ignorance."[14]

[4] *Gn* 44.
[5] *Pr Prol* 58ff.
[6] *Pr Prol.*
[7] Jn 8.34.
[8] Cf. Prov 17:2.
[9] Cf. 1 Cor 4.1.
[10] Cf. 1 Cor 3.2.
[11] Cf. Heb 5.12.
[12] *In Prov* 17.2: Géhin 153.
[13] Cf. Eph 3.18.
[14] *Gn* 36.

Similarly also with the doctrine of God's providence, at which "nearly all are scandalized" and on which, for that reason, one should meditate alone for oneself, as Evagrius learned from his famed contemporary Didymus the Blind.[15]

Evagrius here touches on the questions related to the "judgment" and "providence" of God. The former is concerned with questions of the origin and fall of souls—topics whose *consequences* we admittedly know,[16] but concerning whose causes the Scriptures have revealed nothing to us.[17] Because of our human capacity, neither should we attempt to comprehend them at all;[18] nor, for that reason, then, should we make any binding statements on the subject.[19] The latter relates to the complicated ways in which God, who indeed "wills that all men be saved and come to the knowledge of the truth,"[20] reconciles his creation to himself at the end of time—teachings at which, at all times, "nearly all are scandalized."

> "They will have much joy who love your law, and there is no scandal in them": If the "little ones" are scandalized (and it is written concerning them: "he who scandalizes one of these little ones. . . ."[21]), but those who love the Lord are not scandalized, then the "little ones" will not love the Lord. Thus, they will also not recognize the meaning of things that happen (through God), about which they should, however, be scandalized.[22]

What the "little ones" in true divine love are scandalized by is, as already at the time of Jesus,[23] the unfathomable love of the

---

[15]*Gn* 48.

[16]*In Eccl.*

[17]KG 2.64, 69; 6.1.

[18]*In Prov* 17.2: Géhin 153.

[19]Cf. G. Bunge, "Praktike, Physike und Theologike als Stufen der Erkenntnis bei Evagrios Pontikos," *Ab Oriente et Occidente: Gedenkschrift für Wilhelm Nyssen,* ed. M. Schneider and W. Berschin (St. Ottilien, 1996), 59–72.

[20]1 Tim 2.4.

[21]Mt 18.6 [The ellipsis is the translator's, mainly to draw out that Bunge is leaving the second part of the Biblical passage unsaid, though implied, namely: "It were better for him to tie a mill stone around his neck and be cast into the sea."]

[22]77 *in Ps* 118.165.

[23]Cf. Lk 15.1ff., more commonly.

Father,[24] who accepts not only the "righteous, who need no redemption,"[25] but rather, since he is the "Father of all,"[26] in his mercy he makes even those "unworthy of his providence"its subjects.[27] That seems scandalous to many, because they do not trust that God knows how to find the ways and means "to make friends out of enemies"[28] for himself, whether it be in this age or the one to come. But he whom God truly loves must nurture the same will for salvation as he does[29] and may not, therefore, preclude from his love even the worst of sinners.[30] Moreover, he will love this "fallen image" of God defiled by demons "nearly as much as the original image," Christ![31]

The "depth of the riches of the wisdom and knowledge of God" and his "inscrutable judgments and unsearchable ways,"[32] in which the inscrutable love of the Father reveals itself to his creatures, filled Paul with awe and inspired him with promises full of mysteries.[33] What wonder, then, that the mystics of every age chiefly gave themselves over to the contemplation of these mysteries—not out of vain inquisitiveness,[34] however, but impelled by divine love.

*

Even if the gnostic speaks about these themes, here he will more than ever keep himself from indiscretions, and above all from bald and rash allegations, since misunderstandings can be disastrous for both sides.

> "The just will check his words with judgment": One should avail himself of these words against those who unthinkingly and without the ability to discriminate draw out the mysteries of the Holy

---

[24]*Ep.Mel.* 14.
[25]Cf. Lk 15.7.
[26]Eph 4.6.
[27]*KG* 2.59.
[28]20 *in Ps* 9.37–38; 5 *in Ps* 91.10, more commonly.
[29]*Gn* 22.
[30]50 *in Ps* 118.113.
[31]*Pr* 89.
[32]Rom 11.33, cf. 5 in Ps 118.7.
[33]Cf. Rom 11.25–27.
[34]Cf. *in Eccl* 6.10–12: Géhin 52.

Scriptures. Paul says also: "We should be seen thus: as servants of Christ and stewards of the mysteries of God."[35]

He who does otherwise "gives what is holy to dogs and casts pearls before swine":[36] that is to say, before men who are not yet of "pure heart," but are captive to crude passions and who are, for that reason, incapable of grasping things that go beyond their understanding, for "wisdom enters not a vicious soul, nor dwells in a body that indulges in sin."

Christ's warning here that the "swine," in their irrationality, could "trample underfoot" these pearls while the dogs could "turn and rip you apart" remains unstated. In other words, he who neither is a contemplative nor has access to the "words of the wise," which could properly enlighten him about these matters, has slander ready at hand against him who writes about these things.[37]

But these "mysteries of God" are inaccessible not only to him who is entangled in crude passions, which is patently obvious; but also those who attempt to lay hold of it by means of the simple "external wisdom" of this world and its "dialectic," which perhaps rules them completely, will forever also be barred from it.

> The kingdom of heaven has no need of any soul versed in dialectic, but of a contemplative one. For one finds dialectic also in tainted souls, and contemplation on the contrary only in pure souls. . . . So disregard dialectic, since it is of no use to us on our way. . . . The kingdom of heaven consists not in the word, but in power.[38] The purity of the soul, however, that comes about on the basis of love is called "power"![39]

Evagrius can therefore confidently establish that those things that he experienced from the fathers (and that he, as far as they are suitable to be passed on to others, presented in veiled speech in his *Kephalaia Gnostika*), "will be clear" to those who "have followed the footsteps (of

[35]4 in Ps 111.5, cf. 1 Cor 4.1.
[36]Mt 7.6, cf. *Pr Prol* [9]; *in Prov* 23.9: Géhin 253; idem 26.6: Géhin 320.
[37]*KG* 5.90.
[38]1 Cor 4.20.
[39]*Ep* 62.1f., cf. *KG* 4.90.

the forebears),"[40] since their heart has become pure and contemplative on this "way." He can settle for simply hinting at the existence of these things.

> It is right to converse with young and worldly people about right behavior [i.e., praxis], and to present to them, as far as necessary, the teachings of nature as well as those of theology [at least] in part, without which "no one will see the Lord."[41]

Evagrius, along with Didymus the Blind,[42] advises that we should meditate internally on those things about which we cannot speak with everyone at any arbitrary time. Likewise, we should discuss them in the circle of those "who have been made worthy of knowledge" (of the gnostic,[43] that is) in accordance with their rules;[44] we should do so with that symbolic imagistic speech that Evagrius consistently used with regard to these questions. Those people "made worthy of knowledge" by God also know how to distinguish revealed truth of the Scriptures from that which, precisely because not revealed, is the subject of "investigation."[45] As the concluding line shows, the *Kephalaia Gnostika* is a veritable repertoire of those kinds of "open" questions.

*

To conclude, there is yet an aspect to be pointed out that does not concern the relationship of master to student, but rather entails a fundamental challenge to both the teacher and the student. It has become fashionable today to put ways or means into the hands of anyone with a craving to achieve a "personal experience of God," often without any particular effort. Lecture courses, workshops, and an immense flood of applicable literature give the impression that it really is up to us what kind of experience of God we are to have, and how deep. Without wishing to call into question the fact that many are inspired by a true

[40] *Pr Prol* 6of.
[41] *Gn* 13, cf. Heb 12.14.
[42] *Gn* 48.
[43] *KG* 4.27.
[44] *KG* 4.21.
[45] Cf. Bunge, "Praktike, Physike und Theologike als Stufen der Erkenntnis bei Evagrios Pontikos."

yearning for a God who is curiously "distant," we suspect, in light of the ancient fathers' strict restraint regarding this subject, that it is all too often about a self-induced state of consciousness, rather than a real experience of God. This danger was well known to the ancients, as the following warning teaches:

> Just as it does not help those who suffer with an eye disease to look at length at the blazing and burning sun with naked eyes, so neither does it help the passionate and impure intellect to imitate the reverence of intercessory and sublime prayer "in spirit and truth." Entirely to the contrary, he will irritate the Godhead all the more and cause indignation.[46]

In this chapter of the famous treatise *On Prayer*, spiritual discretion appears as a form of self-discipline. It protects us from a simple "feeling" for things about which we have merely read in others, but that we have never experienced ourselves. This imitation, which ultimately represents a falsification (*anatypōsis*) of true experience, is the death of all spiritual life, since it is entirely untruthful.

For everything in this putative "prayer in spirit and truth" is false: its portrait of God and mankind is no better than its imagined "experience." God is "person" in the absolute sense, and that means he is absolutely free. No one, and especially not any method, can have him at one's disposal. His created image, the human being, is himself a person thanks to this existential reference: openness, "receptivity" (Evagrius says explicitly[47]) of the *I* to an entirely transcendental *Thou*.

The "prayer in spirit and truth" is an absolutely free event between persons, "without any mediation,"[48] since God the Father himself here presents the mediation to God in the form of his Holy Spirit and his only-begotten Son.[49] Such an event cannot be expressed in human terms (for that reason Evagrius only speaks about it in biblical images) and consequently cannot be unilaterally brought about by man as recipient, nor be arbitrarily "imitated." It happens if God "reveals"

---

[46]*Or* 146.
[47]*KG* 6.73.
[48]*Or* 3.
[49]*Or* 59, 60.

himself to his creation: "Prayer is a condition of the intellect that comes about only through the light of the Holy Trinity."[50]

When Evagrius speaks about this unmediated encounter with God, he avails himself of a wholly specific vocabulary. In their own way, the persons of the Holy Trinity "appear"[51] in the spirit of the one praying; they "manifest"[52] themselves to him or "seek him at home."[53] We must "go immaterially to the immaterial" to grasp what this means![54]

[50]Sk 27. Cf. for the following Bunge, *Geistgebet*, chapter VI.
[51]*M.c.* 40.
[52]*Or* 52. *Ep* 58.3.
[53]*Or* 63, 70.
[54]*Or* 67.

CHAPTER X

Gnosis versus Gnosticism

Gnosticism is an ancient, many-layered phenomenon, and not a heresy in the conventional sense. It is therefore also not limited to Christianity; in fact, it is likely of pre- and extra-Christian origin. Many non-Christian religions are gnostic, either in their basic formulation or in their highest philosophical form. At their root lies a rather particular mentality: the conviction that only through knowledge can salvation be achieved. For that reason, Gnosticism is tacitly anthropocentric to the core. Thus, what astounded the first Christians about the manifold manifestations of this oldest and likely also final nemesis of the Church is primarily its absolute capriciousness. "For there will be a time when they will not suffer sound doctrine, but will provide teachers for themselves according to their cravings for their itching ears; and they will turn their ears from truth and turn to fables."[1]

The truth of sound doctrine and the whims of concocted fables are irreconcilably at odds. Admittedly, both have their "teachings" and their "teachers." But if "sound doctrine" is that "sound word" that the "teachers" whom Christ himself set up (namely, the apostles) passed on, and that is "preserved as a magnificent, entrusted good by the Holy Spirit indwelling us,"[2] then that "falsely so-called knowledge" of the self-proclaimed "teachers of wisdom," on the other hand, provides nothing other than "unholy old-wives' tales" and "empty prattle."[3] The "words of belief" that have to do with the facts of salvation, are at odds with the "myths"—stories of their own arbitrary invention without any real or, in particular, any historical content; those who are "ailing" are

[1] 2 Tim 4.3f.
[2] 2 Tim 1.13f.; cf. 1 Tim 6.20.
[3] 1 Tim 4.7; cf. 1:4; 6.20; 2 Tim 4.4.

therefore admonished "to recover in faith"[4] by turning away from these "myths" and toward reality.

And so we get to the heart of our problem. It is not about the knowledge of this or that "eternal truth," about the resolution of some deep existential question that men themselves posed and which they seek to represent, in a perhaps poetically evocative yet ultimately arbitrary way, by means of the resources of the "myth." In this craft, Gnosticism became the all-time master. It is about the words of the apostle and faith—in it, a quite particular mentality is expressed. Evagrius, with Clement of Alexandria, defines this faith as follows: "Faith is an immanent good that exists naturally even in those who do not yet believe in God."[5]

Faith as action is to be differentiated from that capacity for belief given in common to all humans in the creative act, since it stems from their likeness to God, their personal directedness to God. Evagrius defines it as "rational consent of the soul's self-determination (*autexousion*)[6] to God, who reveals himself freely."

Faith as action is, in consequence, primarily an event between persons. The person of God, communicating himself in revelation, answers the person of the human being who ventures in faith: "The word of the Lord came to Abraham in a vision: Fear not, Abraham, I am your shield. . . . Abraham believed the Lord and he counted this as righteousness for him."[7]

God, however, not only reveals himself, his existence, which is to be considered a simple fact of faith;[8] that is to say, in scriptural terms, he does not reveal his "name" only, as to Moses on Mount Horeb,[9] but rather he thereby reveals his will as well. This will is the demand and promise of the future, of that which God wills to accomplish with and for the believer. "And the Lord led Abraham out and said: Look

---

[4]Tit 1.13.
[5]*Pr* 81, cf. Clement of Alexandria, *Strom* 7.10.55.
[6]4 *in Ps* 129.5, cf. Heb 11.1.
[7]Gen 15.1; 6; cf. Rom 4.3.
[8]6 *in Ps* 44.6, cf. Heb 11.6.
[9]Ex 3.13–16.

heavenward and count the stars—can you count them? And he promised him: So shall your descendents be."[10]

Faith, then, is a response to God's future-oriented directive, the consent to that which cannot be comprehended.[11] As this allusion to Hebrews 11 implies, knowledge is a fruit of the promise of salvation accepted in faith,[12] whereas instead in every ancient and modern variety of Gnosticism knowledge is consistently the way to salvation. For "friendship" with God grows from existential faith in God, a faith-based response to his word, and finally in doing this word in concrete day-to-day living; friendship with God means true knowledge of God, and knowledge of God is "eternal life"![13] Abraham is here also an example, our "father in faith" and thus the father of all believers, for he also earned the title "friend of God"[14] for that reason.

> "Affluence increases the number of friends, but the poor is abandoned by the friend he has": Spiritual friendship consists in virtue and knowledge of God, by which we bind ourselves together with the holy angels in friendship.... By the same token, Abraham, having become rich in knowledge,[15] also prepared that mystical table for the friends that appeared at midday.... [16]

Nevertheless, this did not become a reality in full until the New Covenant, perhaps with John the Baptist, the friend of the Bridegroom,[17] and with the apostles.

> "You set a table before me in the presence of my oppressors": At first Christ pastures the sheep as a "shepherd,"[18] but nevertheless he calls his friends to the table as a friend. For, says the Redeemer,

---

[10]Gen 15.5.
[11]4 *in Ps* 129.5, cf. Heb 11.1.
[12]Cf. Heb 11.3.
[13]Jn 17.3, cf. 7 *in Ps* 94.11; 4 *in Ps* 137.7.
[14]Jas 2.23.
[15]Gen 25.8: "Abraham died in a ripe old age and rich in days," i.e., in knowledge (cf. *in Prov* 10.27: Géhin 12)
[16]Cf. *in Prov* 19.4: Géhin 189 (cf. Gen 18).
[17]Jn 3.29.
[18]Jn 10.11.

"Henceforth I call you no longer servants, but friends."[19] The fear of God engenders servants; knowledge of the mysteries [of God], by contrast, engenders a friend.[20]

In a magisterial sentence demonstrating his characteristic succinctness and brevity, Evagrius summarized this experience of faith expanding to knowledge.

> Faith:
> The beginning of love;
> The end goal of love:
> Knowledge of God.[21]

"Love" (*agapē*) here encompasses everything that faith contains as an answer to God's directive. For love, the aim of praxis,[22] is indeed the "shoot of dispassion,"[23] that is, freedom from the tyranny of all those descendants of "self-love" (*philautia*) and exclusive friendship for the self, wherein Evagrius recognizes the root of every vice.[24] Where these intellect-befuddling passions rule, there is no love in the Christian sense of the word, and therefore also no true knowledge.[25] Appropriately, therefore, Evagrius also names love the "door of natural knowledge," i.e., of the knowledge of God mediated in the mirror of created nature, through which one enters into "theology," or immediate and personal knowledge of God, and ultimately to eschatological blessedness.[26]

*

For Evagrius, then, there is no true knowledge that does not rest on right faith,[27] or "right faith about the Holy Trinity," as he specifies.[28]

---

[19] Jn 15.15.
[20] 4 *in Ps* 22.5.
[21] *Mn* 3.
[22] *Pr* 84.
[23] *Pr* 81.
[24] *Sk* 53.
[25] Cf. *KG* 4.47; 6.63.
[26] *Pr Prol* [8].
[27] 3 *in Ps* 30.3; 7 *in Ps* 33.9; 11 *in Ps* 44; 8 *in Ps* 105.16; *Ep* 20.2, more commonly.
[28] *Ep* 61.2; cf. *in Prov* 22.28: Géhin 249.

This right faith, which the gnostic is supposed to nourish through his "spiritual teaching," is in Paul a costly "entrusted good."

> Do not throw off the holy teachings on faith,
> which your fathers have laid down.
> Do not abandon the faith of your baptism
> and do not discard the spiritual seal,
> so that the Lord may come into your soul
> and shield you on the day of evil.[29]

Even if false teachers should have "teachings on faith" and "fathers," nevertheless there is in their words neither "wisdom" nor "true light" (of knowledge),[30] since these are not "the Church's holy teachings on faith."[31]

*

The insurmountable opposition between true gnosis and Gnosticism lies, consequently, in the basic formulation itself. For Evagrius knowledge is—again, entirely biblically—the end of the ways ventured on in faith.[32] These "ways," the virtues, establish a certain similarity between creation and Creator, which, according to an ancient philosophical axiom, is the prerequisite of any knowledge; this idea resurfaces in the biblical passage "be perfect as your heavenly Father is perfect."[33]

"I want to love you, Lord, my strength": We recognize love by love and what is just by justice. For like is known by like.[34]

In a passage of a letter cited immediately above, Evagrius adds:

The first[35] and original[36] commandment is love, with which the intellect sees original love, namely, God.[37] Through our love we

[29] *Mn* 124.
[30] *Mn* 126.
[31] 6 *in Ps* 21.15.
[32] 7 *in Ps* 85.11; 6 *in Ps* 94.10; 2 *in Ps* 137.5; *in Prov* 4.10: Géhin 45 etc.
[33] Mt 5.48.
[34] 1 *in Ps* 17.2. Cf. Clement of Alexandria, *Strom* 5.13.2.
[35] Mk 12.29ff.
[36] 1 Jn 2.7 etc.
[37] 1 Jn 4.4; cf. *Ep* 44.2.

see the love of God for us, as is written in the Psalm: "He will teach the meek his ways."[38] "Moses, however, was meeker than all men,"[39] and the Holy Spirit suitably says:[40] "He showed Moses his ways."[41]

We know that God is "original love" not on the basis of private speculations, but of experience. This "knowledge" is in fact the fruit of salvation history accepted in faith. For it teaches us that "God loved us first," as the apostle triumphantly asserts.[42] This love of God for us reveals itself in the "ways of God," the knowledge of which, however, is accessible only to those who themselves have acquired that meek love of God.

> "For the doers of lawlessness have not walked in his ways": If the doers of lawlessness do not walk in the ways of God, then, manifestly, the doers of righteousness walk in the ways of God. Consequently, the ways of God are natural contemplation, in which we will walk if we do righteousness. . . .[43]

"Natural contemplation" is ultimately nothing other than knowledge of the existential law of all created being, that "unfathomable love of the Father"[44] to which everything is due: the creation, preservation, and perfection of every creature.

This love is not, however, so to speak, the "structuring principle" of creation and its history, its hidden logic grasped only in loving; in Christ, "our love,"[45] it has also become personal presence. For the original love of the Father is not some abstract principle, but rather it revealed itself in the dedication to us of his only-begotten Son.[46] All the "ways of God" ultimately lead, therefore, to the one "way," Christ,

---

[38]Ps 24.9.
[39]Num 12.3.
[40]Ps 102.7.
[41]*Ep* 56.3.
[42]1 Jn 4.19.
[43]2 *in Ps* 118.3.
[44]*Ep.Mel.* 14.
[45]*Ep* 40.3.
[46]1 Jn 4.9–10.

who said: "I am the way."[47] "Knowledge of Christ" is therefore the key term of Evagrian spirituality. "Natural contemplation" opens onto "knowledge of Christ" and "knowledge of God."[48]

> "For in you is the fountain of life, in your light will we see light": If the fountain is life, but Christ is life,[49] then the fountain, too, is Christ.[50]

> In natural contemplation we will see God, just as in the knowledge of Christ we will see God (the Father).[51]

*

One of the most important tasks of the true gnostic is to render intelligible the differentiating characteristic traits of Christian gnosis, namely, the fact that they are grounded in God's personhood and, as can be inferred and grounded on that basis, in the divine likeness of creation. True knowledge, therefore, is a process between persons, the initiative for which ultimately lies consistently with God, our Creator and Redeemer. Whereas in Gnosticism self-knowledge is the safest way to the knowledge of God, in Christianity it is exactly the opposite. The intellect could not even know its own nature, unless the Logos and the Spirit, whose "likeness" it is, were to reveal its nature to it by revealing themselves to it.[52]

From this perspective, material creation is, as it were, a symbol of intelligible and bodiless creation.[53] Created beings, for their part (as a common work of the Son and the Spirit, through whom the Father accomplishes everything) are "letters"[54] drawn by God that make his will, that is, his love, "readable"[55] for us, even if indirectly, so to speak.

---

[47]Jn 14.6, cf. *in Prov* 4.10: Géhin 45; 2 *in Ps* 13.3; 13 *in Ps* 17.24; 1 *in Ps* 66.3, more commonly.

[48]1 *in Ps* 14.1.

[49]Jn 14.6.

[50]5 *in Ps* 35.10.

[51]6 *in Ps* 35.10; cf. *KG* 2.90.

[52]*Ep.Mel.* 21.

[53]*Ep.Mel.* 12.

[54]Cf. *KG* 3.57. ["Letters" not as epistles but as letters of the alphabet.—*Ed.*]

[55]*Ep.Mel.* 6.

In order to know God "personally," a personal act of God is necessary, since, paradoxically, God is only knowable through God: the Father through the "mediation" of his Logos and his Spirit.[56]

Thus, God's "breaking in" (*epidēmia*)[57]—his venturing into creation in the Son through the Spirit, even unto its fallen state[58]—must precede the "ascent"[59] of the intellect as a precondition; it must precede the intellect's "going out (*ekdēmia*) to God."[60]

> For "he who descended is also the same who ascended, so that he might fulfill everything."[61] And if he fulfills everything, then we will "all receive from the fullness of Christ, our Redeemer."[62] For the "fullness of Christ"[63] is spiritual knowledge of the bygone and future ages, along with true faith in the Holy Trinity.[64]

This true faith is possible only because the Holy Trinity reveals itself[65] to the intellect, "inclining" to it "as if out of grace."[66] Our faith is the personal act of breaking in by this self-communication of the Trinitarian God, and the free acceptance of that which no man could have ever imagined.

*

The contemplation of creation, therefore of God's economy of salvation, has no other object than divine love, worthy of amazement, an unimaginable wonder.[67] All speculation and talk in metaphorical speech about the *how* of this groundbreaking love which defies imagination is ultimately secondary, and will become meaningless when creation encounters the Creator himself.[68]

[56] *Ep.Mel.* 18f. 31.
[57] *Ep.fid.* 4.20, more commonly.
[58] Cf. *Ep.Mel.* 56ff.
[59] *Or* 36.
[60] *Or* 47.
[61] Eph 4.10.
[62] Cf. Jn 1.16.
[63] Eph 4.13.
[64] *Ep* 61.2.
[65] *Ep* 61.3.
[66] *Ep* 29.3.
[67] Cf. *Ep.Mel.* 5ff.
[68] *In Eccl* 1.2: Géhin 2.

So, there is no need for those complex speculations about mythical aeon generations and other esoteric "mysteries." Preferable instead is the plain and infinitely simple truth—simple, at any rate, for him who has internalized that "God is love" and created everything out of love, preserves everything, and ultimately leads everything to consummation.[69] The truth is also that love is a gift, a gift for individual being, and that this being is never-ending and blissful communion with the Giver.[70]

This suprarational knowledge given by God as internalization of the truth of faith is a fruit of the salvation already obtained by faith, and never-ending bliss.[71] Conversely, not knowing is the fruit of a personal turning away from God.[72]

By contrast, in Gnosticism every shade is knowledge, as we saw, even the way of salvation of the searching human being, who, nevertheless, does not want to let himself be "found" by God and who in his self-empowerment thinks he has no need of faith. He sees the cause of his misery in not knowing, which he seeks to overcome by recourse to himself.

Such a person, to be sure, seeks "eternal truth," the foundation of all being, but he wishes ultimately to understand it as impersonal, despite his being a "person" himself. For him, the foundation of all being ultimately coincides with the foundation of individual being, without any dialectical tension whatsoever. That great "awakening" for which Gnosticism strives is only an "awakening to oneself"; its knowledge means, therefore, no step over and above this self.

Such a self-imprisonment can never justify the existence, the being, the right to exist, of a *thou* as an *other* self of absolute worth. A sigh of ancient tragedy hangs over this impassioned self-searching.

With all that said, we should not deny to the great sages of old and new Gnosticism the high ethical dignity that often distinguishes them. Nevertheless, we must deny them humility of faith as free consent to the "inscrutable ways of God" toward us—the recognition that there is

[69]*Ep.Mel.* 27ff.
[70]*Ep.Mel.* 62ff.
[71]*Ep.fid.* 12.9–18.
[72]*KG* 1.49.

no other way to God than that which he himself took toward us: Christ. God teaches these "ways," however, to the meek[73] alone, to those who are ready, like God himself, to give place to the mystery of the "other."

*

We have already seen that this humility of faith manifests itself in manifold ways, and also concretely in the attitude toward the sources of knowledge. For the true gnostic, these sources are the Holy Scriptures and the doctrine of the Church, which preserves both. The Church is that place where God permanently stepped into history through the gift of the Holy Spirit and is eternally present through his Word. The restriction to the Spirit-inspired words of the Scriptures is at odds with the cosmopolitanism of Gnosticism as concerns the sources of revelation. For Evagrius applies really harsh words to the "external wisdom" and the "wise of this world standing outside."[74]

> "The lawless told me nonsense, unlike your law, O Lord": Let each one avail himself of this phrase against those who, starting from the external wisdom, take it upon themselves to teach about the knowledge of God.[75]

For it is "better to have a bit of spiritual knowledge than an abundance of the wisdom of the gentiles."[76] Even less can "external wisdom," like "dialectic,"[77] therefore be a source of "true knowledge" for Christians.

> "So I came into your sanctuary, to see your power and your majesty, for better than life is your mercy": The "life" of men means holy knowledge; the "mercy of the Lord," on the other hand, means natural contemplation. Many wise men of this age offer (their) knowledge to us, yet "better than life is the mercy of the Lord."[78]

---

[73]Ps 24.9.
[74]7 *in Ps* 83.11.
[75]37 *in Ps* 118.85.
[76]12 *in Ps* 36.16; cf. 6 *in Ps* 83.11.
[77]Cf. *Ep* 62.1; *KG* 4.90.
[78]2 *in Ps* 62.3–4; cf. *KG* 1.73.

Evagrius, as a monk, goes so far as to designate the demand to learn the "wisdom of the Greeks" as the demon's temptation through vanity.[79] Accordingly, he precludes the possibility that those "wise of this world" could have arrived at true knowledge or wisdom.[80] For their "wisdom" and "knowledge," which Evagrius does not deny that he himself possessed, differs from divine wisdom and knowledge not in degree, but in nature.

> The knowledge that comes to us from without attempts to represent realities through rationales; the knowledge stemming from God's grace, on the contrary, presents the realities to the understanding through one's own witness, whereby the intellect, by looking at them (i.e., the realities), takes their meanings as they come. To the first "manner of knowledge" error is opposed, to the second, however, rage and anger and what follows along with them.[81]

For this distinction, Evagrius relies on his late first teacher, Basil the Great.

> The Cappadocian Basil says that the columns of truth that support "us" are (as knowledge befitting human beings) sustained study and practice, whereas "knowledge" originating from God's grace is righteousness, freedom from anger, and mercy. Those imprisoned by passion may also attain the former, but only the dispassionate are receptive to the latter, i.e., those who, at the time of prayer, see in the intellect their own light's radiance emanating from them.[82]

As we saw, however, prayer in its highest form is an unattainable event, since it "is a condition of the intellect that comes about only through the light of the Holy Trinity."[83]

The knowledge that devolves on us from without, through the mediation of human beings, is a matter of intellectual accomplishment, or of "dialectic," as Evagrius says. Whoever possesses this accomplishment is

[79]*Ant* 7.37.
[80]*KG* 6.22.
[81]*Gn* 4.
[82]*Gn* 45.
[83]Sk 27.

able to procure for himself this "knowledge," or better yet, this "know-how," regardless of how it is constituted around him. Only logical errors stand in his way—technical failures, so to speak. Such a type of impersonal "know-how" is accessible even to the demons.[84]

Entirely different is the case with true knowledge! It has, first and foremost, "arisen from God's grace," that is, it emanates already in the attempt at a personal relationship with the personal origin of reality. For indeed, grace is possible only between persons. It does not rest, therefore, on the structure of words, or on the structure of the terms of dialectic, but on the witness of one's own eyes (*autopsei*); it rests on the unmediated vision of reality. Finally, it is accessible only to those who have laid hold of its corresponding purity, that is, to those who have internally become similar to the truth for which they strive.

*

The defect of highhandedness always clings to external wisdom and knowledge, regardless of how profoundly they might wish to excuse themselves. This highhandedness of human beings, in being satisfied with itself, ultimately seeks only itself.

On the contrary, true wisdom and knowledge are the fruit of the intimate relationship and, indeed, of the "friendship" (*philia*)[85] between man and God. They are reserved for those who, free from every self-ish passion "at the time of prayer," in that glimpse of the highest, unmediated encounter between Creator and creature, "see the radiant light proper to their intellect." "Light" here, as is always the case with Evagrius in this context, is a symbol of knowledge.[86] The "radiant light proper to the intellect" is the capacity for knowledge given to it at creation. In other words, man comes to be inside himself in this glimpse of grace, inside his own being, which is pure "receptivity" to God and his knowledge.[87]

---

[84]*KG* 6.2.

[85]4 *in Ps* 22.5.

[86]Evagrius here cites more commonly Hos 10.12: "Light a light of knowledge for yourselves."

[87]*KG* 6.73.

Here the true gnostic proves to be a true mystic, as one who, in the encounter with the "blissful light of the Holy Trinity," comes to be inside "his own light," that is, his divine likeness as pure reference to God. For "prayer is a condition of the intellect that comes about only through the light of the Holy Trinity."[88] The "true supplicant" and "theologian,"[89] who "prays to the Father in spirit and truth"—that is, in his Holy Spirit and his only-begotten Son[90]—experiences the fact that a man cannot come to himself in any other way, for he encounters the personal foundation of his own being, the triune God of revelation.

[88]Sk 27.
[89]*Or* 61.
[90]*Or* 59. Cf. *Or* 60.

CHAPTER XI

Arcane Discipline versus Esotericism

Gnosis and Gnosticism both have to do with the mysteries of created being, although the questions posed, as well as the answers, are fundamentally different. Gnosticism, which feels bound to no concrete salvation history, takes as the point of departure an existential feeling of foreignness in a deeply enigmatic world. Clement of Alexandria aptly summarizes this existential feeling in a quote from a work of Theodotus, a Gnostic from the school of Valentinus:

> What were we,
> what have we become?
> Where were we,
> where have we been flung?
> Whither do we hasten,
> whence are we freed?
> What is birth,
> what is re-birth?[1]

To these questions Gnosticism, whose self-reference in these questions is rather clearly counterproductive, promises to give an answer. Its "mystery" is the message of liberation of our naturally divine "self" from the entanglement of matter; its "way of salvation" is the knowledge of the causes of this entanglement in the material world, which is the work of a deeply evil "Demiurge," the God of the Old Testament; its gospel is the message of a "foreign God," the Father of Christ, who is himself, however, a mythical being. Ultimately, therefore, "redemption" is liberation from this sense of being "flung" that we owe to our historical situation.

---

[1]Clement of Alexandria, *Excerpta ex Theodoto* 78.2.

*

In opposition to this myth, which is deeply hostile to the body and creation, the Church has always held firmly to the oneness of Creator and Redeemer, and thereby also to the oneness of the Old and New Testaments. The God of the Old Testament, the Creator, is also the Father of Jesus Christ. Thus reality does not go back to two "principles," one good and one evil; rather, all reality, both visible and invisible, has only one author[2] who "in Wisdom made all things,"[3] as Evagrius often repeats.[4] "Nothing is opposed to the first Good, since it is essentially [good], and nothing is opposed to essence (*ousia*)."[5]

And yet evil, even if not originally so,[6] is a reality. Where does it come from, then? Since "God is not the cause of evil, but is the source of good,"[7] the cause of evil is to be sought among creatures.[8] It goes back to a self-inflicted "deliberate choice" (*prohairesis*) of evil instead of ([what would have been] in keeping with their original being)[9] good,[10] an event whose grounds are, nevertheless, beyond our comprehension.[11]

Our historical situation in space and time is due to this meta-historical act, of which we know only through its consequences.[12] This situation is grounded in a "just judgment" of God; it is not, therefore, the expression of a senseless "flungness"; quite to the contrary, God designates it as "wise." In it his benevolent providence manifests itself—the providence that prepared everything necessary for the attainment of virtue and knowledge,[13] and thereby everything necessary for our salvation.

---

[2] Col 1.16; cf. Jn 1.3. The Creed underscored especially this fundamental doctrine.
[3] Ps 103.4.
[4] Cf. *KG* 1.14; 2.70; 3.81; 5.51.
[5] *KG* 1.1.
[6] *KG* 1.40. Cf. Wis 14.13.
[7] *In Eccl* 1.13: Géhin 4.
[8] *KG* 1.2.
[9] *KG* 1.39.
[10] *In Eccl* 6.10–12: Géhin 52.
[11] *In Prov* 17.2.
[12] *In Eccl* 6.10–12: Géhin 52.
[13] 8 *in Ps* 138.16.

Christian gnosis, therefore, does not pose its questions itself, but receives them from creation and salvation history, from the salvific work of God in his creation, as the Holy Scriptures testify. As an example, a list of questions is cited below concerning the "judgment" of God over his creation, that is, the "separation" and differentiation of creatures as God's answer to the free decision of the will of each and every intelligible creation, to which the world owes its situation.[14]

> "I will laud in uprightness of heart, when I have learned the decrees of your righteousness"[15]: He praises God in uprightness of heart who has learned from the Lord the meanings (*logoi*) with respect to the decree:

> For which reason, "the heaven of heaven belongs to the Lord, but the earth he gave to the children of mankind."[16]

> And what the meaning of the demons "beneath the earth"[17] is,

> and why they did not become men,[18]

> what the cause of Hades is, and what paradise is,[19]

> and what is beyond the "Jerusalem above"[20] and its Zion,[21] whence, as it says, Christ comes. For it is written: "From Zion will the Redeemer come, and he will turn godlessness away from Jacob,"[22]

> and what is the meaning of the fallen Israel and the heathens introduced in his place,[23]

[14]Cf. *in Prov* 17.2: Géhin 153; *in Eccl* 6.10–12: Géhin 52.

[15]Ps 118.3.

[16]Ps 113.24.

[17]Phil 2.10.

[18]Cf. *KG* 4.11, as well as *in Eccl* 6.10–12: Géhin 52.

[19]Cf. 7 *in Ps* 9.18 and *KG* 6.8; 3 *in Ps* 21.7; cf. also 2 Cor 2.4.

[20]Gal 4.26, cf. *Ep* 57.4.

[21]6 *in Ps* 13.7 (Zion is a symbol of the Father); cf. also *KG* 5.88; 6.49 (Zion as a symbol of the Holy Trinity and knowledge of it).

[22]Rom 11.26; cf. Is 59.20.

[23]Rom 11.11f.

for which reason not all men were called from the beginning, in
that they accepted the law of Moses, but rather, we became the
(inheritance-) lot of the angels,[24] but Israel became "the portion
of the Lord and the allotment of his inheritance,"[25]

how it came about that the inheritance of the angels believed, but
the "portion of the Lord" remained unbelieving,[26]

and why now even David says: "Your decrees are a large abyss,"[27]

and why Paul says:[28] "O! the depth of the riches of the wisdom
and knowledge of God! How inscrutable are his judgments and
untraceable his ways."[29]

As one can see, all of these questions indeed derive from the Holy
Scriptures, although the answer to them is not in the revelation, as
Evagrius states outright.[30] The Scriptures have a different task: "What
natural contemplation is, the divine Scriptures did not make known.
How one approaches it by carrying out the commandments and the
true teachings—that it openly taught."[31]

That "carrying out of the commandments," i.e., praxis, together
with right belief and the fundamental truths of revelation (namely,
with respect to the Holy Trinity),[32] leads those who "follow in the steps
of the fathers"[33] step by step toward the "door of natural knowledge," by
which one arrives at *theologia* and, at some point, at "ultimate bliss."[34]
It is this suprarational, intuitive "knowledge" that Evagrius calls *gnosis*
and that God grants to those alone who are worthy of it. This unity of
being and knowledge, of becoming the truth and knowing the truth
(Meister Eckhart), inevitably sets up boundaries.

[24]Deut 32.8.
[25]Deut 32.9.
[26]Cf. Rom 9.14ff.
[27]Ps 35.7.
[28]Rom 11.33.
[29]5 *in Ps* 118.7.
[30]*KG* 2.64, 69.
[31]*KG* 6.1.
[32]Cf. *Ep* 39.3; 40.3; 56.2; 61.2.
[33]*Pr Prol* [9].
[34]*Pr Prol* [8].

"'Mystery' means spiritual contemplation, which eludes the comprehension of many."[35] Intended here is that mystery of "height, breadth, length, and depth," that is, the fact of those "measures" that transcend human comprehension, which subsist between reason-endowed beings (angels, humans, demons), and which Paul did not want to entrust to the immature Corinthians, but rather only to the mature Ephesians.[36]

*

The keys to those "mysteries" are not, however, constituted by an impersonal, eternal "truth," but rather by a person: Christ,[37] who alone knows the "first principle" of all created being.[38] "Knowledge of our salvation,"[39] therefore, is always ultimately "knowledge of Christ," for "in Christ are hidden all the treasures of wisdom and knowledge."[40] These "treasures of wisdom" are generally almost as inaccessible as the "hidden meaning of Scripture," since not everyone can comprehend them.[41]

> "To the end. Concerning the hidden things of the Son. A Psalm of David": The "hidden things" mean the incommunicable[42] knowledge with respect to the mysteries of Christ.[43]

Christ himself (and the Holy Spirit,[44] respectively) reveals to those he finds worthy of them, these mysteries that are not to be divulged.[45] It is thus clearly not about a general teaching of the Church,[46] but rather about those "insights" into the ineffable that have been granted

---

[35] *KG* 6.65.

[36] *In Prov* 17.2: Géhin 153; cf. also *in Eccl* 6.10–12: Géhin 52.

[37] 6 *in Ps* 35.10; 1 *in Ps* 14.1.

[38] *Gn* 40.

[39] *KG* 1.10.

[40] Col 2.2f.

[41] *In Prov* 23.1.3: Géhin 250.

[42] *Aporrhētos* can mean *ineffable* as well as *keeping secret*. Among the philosophers this meant teachings not to be disseminated outside the circle of the school. Concerning such "ineffable knowledge" cf. *KG* 4.66; *Mn* 120; *Ep.Mel.* 67.

[43] 1 *in Ps* 9.1.

[44] 59 *in Ps* 118.131.

[45] Cf. *in Prov* 20.9: Géhin 210; 9 *in Ps* 39.11.

[46] As the title of the Psalm teaches ("To the *end*"), it clearly deals with questions of *eschatology*.

to the mystics of every era since the time of Paul. As the list cited above teaches, the questions themselves derive through and from Scripture (more precisely, from the Pauline epistles) and not from some foreign source, even if Scripture does not answer them.

If things are so, then why does the Christian gnostic nevertheless concern himself with these questions? Because the false gnostics would otherwise monopolize them and endanger the belief of the Church through their wild speculations. For their alleged "answers" to the big existential questions of humankind always come down to the fact that they "throw in the Creator's face that he is unjust or unwise."[47]

In other words, they impute to the "just Judge" that his "decrees," to which the world owes its situation, are the expression of his "partiality."[48] Accordingly, creation and its history would not be pervaded by the "manifold wisdom"[49] of him who "in Wisdom made all things,"[50] since he himself is "essentially wisdom"[51]; rather, it is ultimately the expression of the irrationality of our existence. This "falsely so-called knowledge," deeply hostile to the body and to creation, easily devolves in every age into unrestrained libertinism, which everyone then attempts to justify after his fancy.

*

In his *Kephalaia Gnostika*, primarily intended for "gnostics,"[52] Evagrius addressed many of these questions, very often in deliberately veiled speech. Indeed, he said expressly that he did not "want to communicate everything he saw or heard, but rather only what he learned from the holy fathers, in order to tell it to others."[53]

What applies to the "mysteries of the Holy Scriptures" applies to these questions. One may divulge them neither imprudently nor indiscriminately[54] since, to begin with, one is to guard oneself, following

[47]5 *in Ps* 143.7.
[48]Cf. *in Eccl* 6.10–12: Géhin 52.
[49]Eph 3.10.
[50]Ps 103.24.
[51]3 *in Ps* 138.7; 2 *in Ps* 144.3.
[52]Cf. *KG* 4.21, 27 and the concluding sentence.
[53]Cf *Pr Prol* [9].
[54]4 *in Ps* 111.5.

Christ's phrase, from "giving what is holy to dogs and casting pearls before swine," as we have already seen. Some things are in themselves ineffable and not expressed in the Scriptures, being at best obscurely hinted at. This harkens back to Paul in the third heaven and paradise, and to the "ineffable words" he heard there,[55] which doubtless contained those "mysteries" to which he often alludes without ever communicating them.

But this arcane discipline, which the spiritual father (who for Evagrius is a "wise man" and a "gnostic") is to cultivate, has also another sense. It does not by any means limit itself to the questions referenced above concerning "judgment" and "providence," since they, regardless of the emphasis, play no insignificant role in the realm of theology (in the ancient sense) and in *askēsis*—two areas, then, which for modern sensitivities do not fall under the duty of secrecy.

Evagrius emphatically warns against "theologizing" flippantly, that is, making statements about God and setting up "definitions" about divinity, since such boundaries are commensurate only with the things involved, that is, created things.[56] He who is bound to the material world, and who therefore necessarily derives his terminological apparatus from it, might well risk a false step about God, who is not subject to sense-perceptible realities.[57] Therefore, he who dares to concern himself frequently with "theological" problems despite the weakness of his own intellect, does so at the risk of saying something inaccurate about God and, on account of this godlessness, to lose "spiritual knowledge,"[58] which is precisely that suprarational, intuitive gnosis that is purely the gift of the Spirit.

The only appropriate stance toward the "ineffability" of the mystery of the Holy Trinity is faith[59] and quiet prayer,[60] that is, two acts that are not rationally communicable, but rather existentially incommunicable acts of personal encounter.

---

[55] 2 Cor 12.1ff.
[56] *Gn* 27.
[57] *In Eccl* 5.1–2: Géhin 35.
[58] *In Prov* 25.17: Géhin 310.
[59] *Inst. mon.* 2.33.
[60] *Gn* 41.

*

Yet monastic asceticism also has its arcana. In general, the craving to reveal to others the "mysteries of monastic life,"[61] namely, of one's own ascetic walk,[62] perhaps of one's fasting,[63] is nothing more than the demonic temptation of vanity. In asceticism, the rule runs: "Seal in the pleasant fragrance of your ascetic efforts with silence."[64]

The same goes for anything "that happens to us in our cell, either on the angels' part or that of demons."[65] To make revelations flippantly here is no more than vain thirst for glory. For that reason Evagrius also refuses to publicize certain demonic temptations, such as perhaps that of blasphemy,[66] or paranormal psychosomatic phenomena of grief.[67] The reason is simple: such things would only set up stumbling blocks or discourage beginners and frighten them away. Incidentally, for this duty of silence Evagrius expressly relies on a commandment "of our holy priest," Macarius of Alexandria.[68]

What, then, should we think about an "esoteric" publisher's countless book ads praising a work, just now appearing in its third edition, with the words: "With the knowledge proffered here, which was never before allowed to be unveiled outside the 'inner circle,' anyone can learn. . . . "? He who hastily releases "the ineffable" to the people in a pocket-sized edition really has nothing to say.

*

In arcane discipline and esotericism, fundamentally different attitudes toward gnosis and Gnosticism mirror each other in blatantly obvious ways. "Esoterica" have filled volumes and libraries since antiquity. Their alleged "mysteries" are easily accessible to anyone. Modern workshops promise their paying customers "initiation" into the unimaginable in

[61]A*nt* 7.17.
[62]*Ant* 7.20.
[63]*Ant* 7.32.
[64]*Eul* 14.
[65]*Ep* 16.5.
[66]*Ant* 8.21.
[67]*Ant* 4.72.
[68]*M.c.* 37; cf. also *M.c.* 16.

the shortest time. This is a repulsive indiscretion, for as Paul noted,[69] an absolute arbitrariness of whole swarms of "masters" characterizes this growing longing for "itching ears."

None of that is found in true gnosis. Here, the arcana of revelation are in principle accessible to anyone baptized into faith. For "mysticism" is nothing other than a humble, quiet internalization of theology on the arduous way of praxis. Christian gnosis is thereby ultimately an expression of reverence before God and one's neighbor.

Christian gnosis is reverence before God, about whom our bounded spirit, which is in every way tied to the sensible world, can know no more than what he himself wills to communicate about himself in revelation. But it is also reverence for God's creation, whose destiny its Author alone determines, and whose mysteries he alone makes accessible to those who have become similar to his heart.[70]

It is, finally, reverence for one's neighbor and for his potential, a loving consideration for his own internal maturation process. This aspect is ultimately decisive for that arcane discipline, practiced not by Evagrius alone. To quote Maximus the Confessor:

> The teachers of the Church, who knew how to make much of this passage[71] on the grounds of the grace conferred upon them, deemed it wiser to revere it with silence; for the spirit of the many did not seem to them to be ready to comprehend the depth of these words.[72]

[69]2 Tim 4.3f.

[70]Cf. Mt 11.29.

[71]Intended here is Gen 2.9.

[72]*Questions to Thalassios* 43 (PG 90.412A). The [German] translation is by H. U. von Balthasar, *Kosmische Liturgie* (Einsiedeln, 2nd edition, 1961), 357, who cites other pertinent passages in the entry here provided. Besides his own noteworthy reflections in the entry here provided, cf. also his highly controversial book: *Was dürfen wir hoffen?* (Einsiedeln, 1986). Let it be noted that with respect to this question, Evagrius expressed himself with much more reserve than his modern interpreter and critic. [*Translator's note*: Bunge's German text reproduces Hans Urs von Balthasar's own translation of Maximus' underlying Greek. I have based my own translation on von Balthasar's German text as reproduced here by Bunge, rather than the available translation of *Kosmische Liturgie* masterfully rendered into English by Brian Daley. See Hans Urs von Balthasar, *Cosmic Liturgy: The Universe According to Maximus the Confessor*, Brian Daley, trans. (San Francisco, CA: Ignatius Press, 2003).]

CHAPTER XII

Spiritual Mystagogy

T he Gnosticism of every age vaunts itself not only for knowing how to enact hidden mysteries, but also for having "initiates" who may initiate others into these mysteries. We have already seen what Evagrius thinks about these "wise men of this world" and their "external wisdom."

Misuse, however, is no excuse for throwing the baby out with the bathwater. Since olden times, the Church has also known a "mystagogy," an initiation into the mysteries of the faith: the catechumenate and baptismal instruction. One of the most beautiful patristic texts, the *Mystagogical Catechesis* of Cyril of Jerusalem,[1] is dedicated to this "initiation." No wonder, then, that monasticism, which understands itself as a "second baptism" in the flood of tears of repentance, developed a typology aspiring to deepen the path of Christian initiation through a renewed commitment. The topic has many ramifications that exceed the scope of this little book. Thus, it is hinted at only in outline in order to determine once more the theological locus of spiritual fatherhood.

*

The central salvific events to which the people of the Old Testament owe their existence are those described from the departure from Egypt to the entrance into the Promised Land. "They, however, experienced these things by way of prefiguration,"[2] i.e., they are not constrained in their historical reality, but rather are open as a "prefiguration" to an outstanding "fulfillment," namely, that which is accomplished "in the fullness of time" in Christ. Scripture, which reports these Old Testament salvific happenings, is therefore to be taken typologically, as Paul

[1] It likely stems from his successor, John II.
[2] 1 Cor 10.11.

extensively did. The ancient Church followed him in this regard, and with it, of course, Evagrius also.[3]

"When you are seated at the table of a ruler for a meal, understand intelligibly what is laid before you": One must understand the divine Scripture intelligibly, for the knowledge that follows from history (i.e., in the literal sense) is not true.[4]

It is not "true" with respect to reality because it embeds in the past what transpired. Only an "intelligible and spiritual understanding" that tends to the "hidden meaning"[5] not accessible to all—to the spiritual content, which is inspired by the Holy Spirit—opens what transpired to its completion which as yet lies in the future, and which is given only with the coming of Christ.

Paul already understood the "spiritual rock" that poured water forth for the people of Israel in the desert in this sense: "but this rock was Christ."[6] Thus, the Church from the very beginning pointed the events of the exodus toward their fulfillment in Christ. Since "spirituality" is nothing but internalized theology, Evagrius can construe the same salvific event yet again "intelligibly and spiritually" and signify the inner spiritual path the baptized person is to forever pursue afresh, since, to be sure, it runs through the ascetical life. He then draws the big picture: "Egypt means vice, desert praxis, the land of Judah contemplation of the bodily, Jerusalem of the bodiless, and Zion is a symbol of the Trinity."[7]

This symbolism, which is found in all the writings of the Pontic monk, is accordingly elucidated as need arises. Because of the chosen people's 430 years of absence from their own land, Egypt is always a symbol "of this world" (of sin),[8] and thus of evil;[9] Pharaoh, who held

---

[3]Cf. G. Bunge, "Der mystische Sinn der Schrift: Anlässlich der Veröffentlichung der Scholien zum Ecclesiasten des Evagrios Pontikos," *Studia Monastica* 36 (1994): 135–146.

[4]*In Prov* 23.1: Géhin 251. Cf. 9 *in Ps* 118.18.

[5]*In Prov* 23.1, 3: Géhin 250. As a survey of the Evagrian corpus shows, the adjective *mystikos* never has here the meaning of "mystic" in the modern sense, but rather means simply "hidden," and thereby not generally accessible. In this sense our article mentioned in footnote 3 above is to be corrected.

[6]1 Cor 10.4.

[7]*KG* 6.49.

[8]12 *in Ps* 104.22.

[9]*KG* 5.88; cf. 3 *in Ps* 135.6; 19 *in Ps* 67.32.

the people in slavery, is a prefiguration of the devil.[10] The exodus is thus the "departure from vice and ignorance,"[11] the entrance into the "Promised Land" a symbol of the knowledge of God, and his creation[12] a symbol of the entrance into knowledge.[13]

Guided by the pillar of "cloud" and "fire" (a symbol itself of the holy and intelligible angelic powers) and led by Moses and Aaron, the people of God accomplished in their forty-year wandering the "departure from vice to virtue,"[14] and finally, under Joshua, the "entrance from virtue to knowledge" as well.[15]

By transposing, and thereby internalizing, this salvific event to the plane of the spiritual life of the individual Christian, those forty years in the desert, during which Israel "hungered and thirsted and was tempted," become for Evagrius a symbol of praxis,[16] that "spiritual method which purifies the passionate part of the soul."[17] This transpires through the "practice" of the commandments.[18] Only he who has spent this "time in the desert" successfully may thereby cross the "Jordan" and take possession of the "palm city" of Jericho,[19] and afterward also take part in the division of the promised land among the twelve tribes.[20]

He who comes into this "promised land," which is accessible only to the "meek,"[21] finds himself henceforth in the realm of knowledge or contemplation, that second stage of the spiritual life. In this "land," however, there are different regions for the tribes, each of which, of course, has its own symbolic meaning.[22]

---

[10]12 *in Ps* 104.22; cf. 3 *in Ps* 135.6.
[11]*In Prov* 1.20–21: Géhin 12; cf. idem 8.3: Géhin 99.
[12]*In Prov* 17.2: Géhin 153. Cf. 3 *in Ps* 135.6 more commonly.
[13]2 *in Ps* 120.8.
[14]15 *in Ps* 76.21.
[15]2 *in Ps* 120.8; cf. *Ep* 58.2; *KG* 5.47; *in Prov* 17.2: Géhin 153.
[16]*KG* 6.49; 3 *in Ps* 135.6; cf. *in Prov* 21.19: Géhin 227.
[17]*Pr* 78.
[18]*Pr* 81.
[19]*M.c.* 20.
[20]*In Prov* 17.2: Géhin 153.
[21]9 *in Ps* 36.11 (cf. Mt 5.5); *in Prov* 25.25: Géhin 316.
[22]*In Prov* 17.2: Géhin 153 (cf. Jos 13.7).

In the middle of this land lies Jerusalem, "translated"[23] according to ancient etymology as "vision of peace."[24] The city itself is a symbol for "natural contemplation,"[25] that is, the knowledge of created nature. In the middle of this holy city, again, there is the "lofty mountain"[26] of Zion, symbol of the knowledge of the Holy Trinity.[27]

If we look more closely, we also discover in it a symbol of the Father,[28] who in accordance with his nature is the personal source of his Son and Spirit; in accordance with grace, however, he is also the personal source of created natures.[29] That is why, with respect to Christ, the saying goes: "the Redeemer comes from Zion,"[30] whereby the entire vast horizon of the salvific economy of God and, thereby, of the "knowledge of Christ," opens itself up to the contemplatives.

The symbolism, however, is by no means exhausted thereby, since according to ancient etymology "Zion" is translated as "watch post,"[31] and since in the Holy Scriptures the phrase goes God "lives in Zion."[32] "Zion" can also mean the "light-like intellect,"[33] the "seer"[34] and "temple of the Holy Trinity"[35] in which the divinity, so to speak, "dwells."[36]

*

In the individual events of the departure from Egypt, of the forty years in the desert, and finally of the entrance into the Promised Land, a path of an ever deeper initiation into the mystery of the Holy Trinity is delineated for spiritual understanding. It leads from purification from

[23]Cf. Heb 7.2.
[24]1 *in Ps* 147.13.
[25]*KG* 5.88; cf. 6.49.
[26]*Ep* 58.4.
[27]*KG* 6.49; cf. 5.88.
[28]6 *in Ps* 13.7; 5 *in Ps* 118.7.
[29]*Ep.Mel.* 25.
[30]Rom 11.26; cf. Is 59.20.
[31]1 *in Ps* 86.2; 1 *in Ps* 147.13.
[32]Ps 9.12.
[33]*Sk* 25; cf. *Gn* 45; *Or* 74. That the intellect is "light-like" (*phōtoeidēs*) means that it has returned to its original condition as a "knowing substance" (*KG* 1.3), since "light" is a symbol for knowledge.
[34]*KG* 3.30.
[35]*Sk* 34.
[36]*Sk* 25; cf. 2 *in Ps* 86.5; 1 *in Ps* 125.1.

the passions through the mediated knowledge of God by his creation, and to the experience of unmediated "indwelling" of the triune God in the intellect that has itself become "light-like," that is, it has become the Godlike personal essence of Spirit-endowed creation.

Guidance is necessary on this danger-ridden path, as it was at the time of the people of the first covenant, since the fight against the "foreign peoples" of the demons and the passions, who initially occupied, and still occupy the Promised Land,[37] must be guided "with knowledge," that is to say, with insight into the nature of this complex event.[38] In principle God takes over this guidance himself, just as in the Old Testament, yet he constantly exercises it through his messengers in the Old Testament: through his angels, who went before the people in the pillar of cloud and fire;[39] through Moses and Aaron;[40] and finally through Joshua.[41]

In the New Testament, again it is the angels[42] (that is, the personal guardian angel, mentioned above) and perhaps then the apostles, such as Paul,[43] in whom Christ himself speaks.[44] In the life of the individual, it is precisely the spiritual father (as "helper of the angels"[45] and "shield-bearer of wisdom"[46]) in whom Christ speaks. In that they "anoint men for battle and heal the bites of the wild beasts,"[47] "through their spiritual teaching they lead the impure to virtue"[48] and finally to knowledge. Their angel-like service is in imitation of the "father," Christ.[49] For our Redeemer, God the Word, came in order to cast an "intelligible fire" on the earth,[50] that is, his spiritual teaching, so as "to

---

[37]Cf. 6 *in Ps* 134.12 (= *KG* 5.30) more commonly.
[38]*Pr* 50.
[39]20 *in Ps* 104.39.
[40]15 *in Ps* 76.21.
[41]Cf. *KG* 6.47.
[42]Cf. *KG* 6.86 more commonly.
[43]16 *in Ps* 67.30.
[44]*In Prov* 20.9a: Géhin 210.
[45]*KG* 6.90.
[46]*KG* 5.65.
[47]*Pr* 100.
[48]*In Prov* 28.8: Géhin 345; cf. idem 17.17: Géhin 164.
[49]*Ep* 61.1.
[50]Cf. Lk 12.49.

burn" the wicked customs of humans and to "test"[51] the pure in order to guide all creatures finally back to God.[52]

"Praised be God, the Father of our Lord Jesus Christ, who has blessed us in Jesus Christ, our Lord,"[53] and through faith in his Son strengthened us who were shaken, and through his death raised us up who had fallen, and who liberated us from poverty, and delivered us from the hands of the oppressors by sending his holiness here, Christ, our Redeemer and the Giver of the life of our souls, and who gave us daring outspokenness in him by conquering all those powers who opposed us, by saying: "Take heart, for I have overcome the world,"[54] and cast Satan out of us through his holy commandments,[55] and opened the door to life, and pointed out the way of the commandment, that is, he himself became a way for us, as he said: "I am the way,"[56] in order that we, by hastening toward him and through him, might attain the knowledge of the prayer-worthy and Holy Trinity.[57]

[51]2 *in Ps* 49.3; 1 *in Ps* 74.4.
[52]*KG* 4.89.
[53]Eph 1.3.
[54]Jn 16.33.
[55]Cf. Jn 12.31.
[56]Jn 14.6.
[57]*Ep* 60.1.

Discernment of Spirits

To those gifts of the Spirit that characterize the gnostic belongs also that of the "discernment of spirits." It is not also, however, ultimately directed to the person and teaching of the spiritual father himself. For the buzz everywhere is about "spirit" and "spiritual," indeed, "spiritual fatherhood," even in Gnosticism. Yet, what spirit may one trust? The Apostle John says in his first epistle: "Believe not every spirit, but test the spirits."[1]

In the following, a few criteria of this constantly necessary differentiation of the spirits will be named, as they arise from the foregoing chapters.

*

The epithet "spiritual" is on everyone's lips, but what "spirit" is thereby intended, in the unlikely case that the word is not mindlessly employed? Does it refer to the "spirit" of men or to an ungraspable cosmic "spirit"? Or is "spiritual" here simply opposed to "material"? For Evagrius and the tradition he represents, "spiritual" refers consistently to the Holy Spirit.[2] The Holy Spirit is one of the persons of the triune God of revelation, consubstantial with the Father and Son.

To apply the adjective "spiritual" to a person or to his activities therefore means, for Evagrius, also a confession of the mystery of the "holy and prayer-worthy Trinity," and thereby of a personal relationship with God in the Holy Spirit, who is not merely an impersonal "power" or a cosmic "principle." This is clear particularly in mysticism, which in the most authentic and deepest sense is "spirituality"—and here, specifically, it is spirituality in prayer as the authentic locus of the

[1] 1 Jn 4.1.
[2] Cf. Bunge, *Geistgebet*, chapter 4.

experience of God. To pray to the Father "in spirit and truth" means, for Evagrius, to be inducted into the mystery of intra-Trinitarian personal life, beyond anything rationally comprehensible and imaginable.

Thus, "spiritual" in the Christian understanding is only that which lies at the core of and unfolds the belief in the revelation of the Holy Trinity. What is more, for the heart of every Christian (and therefore also of Evagrius), mysticism is the unfathomable mystery of the Trinity.[3] A few examples follow.

*

"Spiritual contemplation" or "beholding" occupies a central place in the thought of the Pontic monk. Its object, so long as man is situated in this space-time world, is at first *creation* in its diversity—"that which came into being" (*ta gegonota*)[4] by God's Spirit and Son.

Thus the spirits part ways again, for "spiritual contemplation," in Christian understanding, may never separate God and world. World is creation, the free establishment of a reality in time through the three eternal persons of God. It is the locus of this self-disclosure of God, and the created spirit indirectly (*analogōs*) beholds in its "beauty" its Creator himself.[5] Being-in-the-world and being-in-the-body are therefore not the consequences of a "cosmic drama" or of a fatal "slungnness," but the expression of God's "judgment and providence," whose sole objective is the salvation of all creatures.

Particularly the body, which is "congeneric" (*syngenēs*) with the world,[6] since "it came into being together with it,"[7] is not in the least a sheer burden, even if Evagrius, following traditional convention, may on occasion call it, a "dungeon." Nevertheless, only he who, owing to his purity, may give himself over to natural contemplation even without the body, may pray with the Psalmist to be delivered from this

---

[3]Cf. G. Bunge, "Mysterium Unitatis: Der Gedanke der Einheit von Schöpfer und Geschöpf in der evagrianischen Mystik," *Freiburger Zeitschrift für Philosophie und Theologie* 36 (1989): 449–469.

[4]Cf. *Ep.fid.* 11.1ff.; *Ep.Mel.* 5ff.

[5]Wis 13.5, cf. *Ep.fid.* 12.35ff.; *Ep.Mel.* 6; 7 *in Ps* 17.12.

[6]Cf. *Ep.fid.* 7.33; 12 *in Ps* 43.20; 5 *in Ps* 83.6–7.

[7]Cf. *KG* 3.26.

"dungeon."[8] For in fact the body is primarily an "instrument" of that mediated knowledge of God, discussed above. Those "meanings" (*logoi*) are now accessible to us through it—those meanings that, like traces of the operation of Spirit and Logos, structure creation spiritually and "logically," and therefore render it comprehensible for us.

Hence, here again an impassable barrier is erected against any form of Manichaean dualism hostile to world and body. His rigorous asceticism notwithstanding, Evagrius is a determined opponent of suicide, regardless of its being a means to escape from the "prison" of the body.[9]

*

These *logoi* or traces[10] of the Logos are accessible to us not only in the "book of creation,"[11] that "book of God,"[12] but also in the inspired "spiritual words" of Scripture, most especially those of the Old Testament. Since it is one and the same Spirit who, in league with the Logos, ensures the unity not only of creation, but also of salvation history, any dualism between one "alien God" of the Old Testament, who is merely just, and the loving "unknown God" of the New Testament, the Father of Christ, is precluded. He who made all things through his Word and his Spirit is also the same who through his Son and Spirit preserves, steers, redeems, and fulfills all things.

With respect to the stance toward the inspiration of the entirety of the Holy Scriptures and the question concerning whose word counts as "Scripture" and source of revelation, true gnosis and those old and new forms of Gnosticism necessarily diverge. What should one make of the carefree cosmopolitanism of Gnosticism, when the saying goes:

> Do not allegorize the words of reprehensible persons, nor look for something spiritual in them. For it may be that God, by (reason of) salvation history, would accomplish something "through them," as

[8]*KG* 4.70 = 5 *in Ps* 141.8.
[9]*KG* 4.33, 76, 83.
[10]Evagrius speaks of "impressing on," cf. 7 *in Ps* 29.8.
[11]*Ep.Mel.* 5ff.
[12]8 *in Ps* 138.16.

in the case of Barlaam[13] and Caiaphas,[14] in order that by the one
the birth and by the other the death of our Redeemer might be
foretold.[15]

The cosmopolitanism of Gnosticism with regard to its sources
of revelation is ultimately no more than the expression of the self-
empowerment of the old Adam, of the compulsion to determine by
himself when and how he "will become like God."[16]

This "being bound by Scripture" of Christianity has a totally different rationale than the estimation of the "holy scriptures" in the different currents of old and new Gnosticism. For history enters into the
place of the timeless Gnostic myth, whereupon shoreless time becomes
the time of God's salvation[17]—that unattainable time of salvation in
which it is no longer insignificant where and when one "experiences
God," as is so commonly said today.

Christian commitment to Scripture is commitment to the historic-
ity of revelation, and thereby to the concrete, indeed, *unique* entering-
in of God into a unique, concrete history determined by him alone.
The "fullness of time" appointed by God brings about a "before" and
an "after" of absolute uniqueness within the inherently directionless
streams of time.[18] "Scripture" is from this perspective much less a "wisdom book," in the extra-Christian sense, than a record of this history
of God with his creation. As such, it definitely reflects for him who
would read it the "manifold wisdom of God" in an incomparable way.
That Evagrius is well aware of this unique character of salvation history
and its salvific events, the following scholion teaches:

"But our God is above in heaven. In heaven and on earth, everything he willed, that too he brought about": Hence we know that
God may do everything he wills. For it says "everything God willed,
that he brought about." Not, however, that he would necessarily

[13]Num 24.17–19.
[14]Jn 11.49–53.
[15]*Gn* 21.
[16]Gen 3.5.
[17]Cf. Heb 1.1ff.
[18]In that respect Evagrius divides time into that which happened "before the coming
of our Redeemer" and that which happens "now," after this event.

will everything he may do. He could make the resurrection of the dead happen now, but he does not will it. And moreover, he may become man, but he does not will it.[19]

*

"Resurrection of the dead" and "becoming man" point to him in whom all the salvific work of God, in the "fullness of time,"[20] once and for all, found an unrepeatable "fullness" and "fulfillment," through which, mysteriously, the "fathers" of the past also retroactively, as it were, attained "perfection":[21] Christ, the incarnate Logos and Son of the Father. For Christian gnosis, the commitment to Christ is therefore no less decisive than that to the mystery of the Trinity.

> He who calls the Holy Trinity
> a creation, blasphemes God,
> and he who repudiates his Christ,
> will not know him.[22]

In the confession of the unity of the figure of Christ, which may not be relegated to a Jesus of history and a Christ of belief, the spirits yet again diverge. Gnosticism sees in Christ no more than a preeminent but ultimately mythical "intermediate being," of which there were others before and of which there will be others in the future. Thereby the historically unique[23] evaporates into the mythically detached. By logical consequence, Christ is thereby now and again also degraded to a simple "cosmic principle." All of this disregards the personhood of divine being. Impersonal cosmic processes may repeat themselves infinitely; only the personal God may carry out unique and effective actions, unique even in space and time. "Truly I say to you: many prophets and righteous men longed to see what you see and did not see it, and to hear what you hear, and did not hear it."[24]

[19] 5 *in Ps* 113.11.
[20] Gal 4.4.
[21] Heb 11.40.
[22] *Mn* 134.
[23] Heb 9.12.
[24] Mt 13.17.

For the Christian gnostic, the "knowledge of Christ" contains for that reason "*all* of the treasures and wisdom and knowledge of God." His "spiritual teaching" leads to nothing other than this mystery.

*

A final and permanent divergence of the spirits takes place in the stance the gnostic takes with respect to the "spiritual seal," that is, to baptism,[25] and thereby to the Church: its teachings, sacraments, and existence in time and eternity. Decisive here is whether or not one takes seriously the historical uniqueness of revelation—and thereby of the personal freedom of God. In other words, the concern here is the recognition that the only way to God is that way which he himself took to us. This "way," Christ, became in the Church a reality enduring until the end of time, accessible and "walkable" to anyone who believes.

Although Evagrius discusses the Church relatively seldom, which is no cause for wonder in a desert father, the corresponding statements are nevertheless altogether clear. Evagrius certainly knows a symbolic meaning of *ekklesia*;[26] and yet, by the "dogmas of the catholic and apostolic Church," with respect to which one should suffer no "shipwreck,"[27] undoubtedly the historical reality of the Church is intended.[28] Similarly, Evagrius laments the division in the Church of his time and celebrates its regained unity.[29] Although there is also no lack of critical observations concerning "shepherds,"[30] especially as pertains to vain striving for the priesthood,[31] not uncommon among monks, nevertheless the phrase unmistakably is:

> He who plunges the Church of the Lord into confusion,
> him will the fire consume,
> he who opposes the priest,
> him will the earth swallow.[32]

[25]*Mn* 124.
[26]3 *in Ps* 45.5; *in Eccl* 1.1: Géhin 1; idem 1.2: Géhin 2.
[27]*In Prov* 24.6: Géhin 266.
[28]Cf. 6 *in Ps* 21.15; 8 *in Ps* 44.10; 8 *in Ps* 91.14.
[29]*Ep* 52.5; cf. *Ep* 24.2.
[30]*In Prov* 26.17: Géhin 326; idem 27.23f.: Géhin 340.
[31]*In Prov* 26.17: Géhin 326; *Ant* 7.8, 26; *M.c.* 28; *Pr* 13.
[32]*Mn* 114. By "priest" he means bishop.

As the clear reference to the Korahites' revolt against Moses and Aaron indicates,[33] this phrase probably plays on the Church division Jerome instigated in Bethlehem against his rightful bishop, John of Jerusalem.[34]

That Church, in the peace of which Evagrius died on Epiphany of 399, is thus not a pure "spiritual Church," nor is it not reserved for the "perfect" alone.

> "Praise [God] with cymbals and choir. Praise him with stringed instruments and flutes": The choir means the agreement of rational souls, who "all" say the same thing and among whom there is no division.

> Stringed instruments mean harmony.

> The flute means the Church of God, which consists of practic and contemplative souls.[35]

The Church is therefore, so to speak, a symphonic orchestra playing in unison, in which the *praktikoi* (on the way to purification from the passions) are to be found on equal footing next to the *theōrētikoi* (just then arrived at the contemplation of the hidden mysteries of God), playing in praise of God. And so the concrete, historical Church is in fact no pure "spiritual Church," which would preclude the "Hylics" imprisoned by matter as something reserved for gnostic "Pneumatics" alone, but rather a colorful mixture of both.

> "The daughters of kings [are there] for your glory, the queen stands at your right hand, dressed in gold-threaded clothes, [arrayed] multifariously": When the holy students attain the kingdom of heaven, they become kings. For that reason, also those souls begotten by them through virtue are called "daughters of kings." All these souls, united in faith and virtue, constitute the queen, who stands at the right hand of Christ. Now the Church of the Lord has gold-threaded clothes, "knowing in part

---

[33]Num 16.
[34]Cf. Bunge, *Briefe*, 60ff.
[35]*5–7 in Ps* 150.4b; cf. *1 in Ps* 86.2; *Mn* 121.

and prophesying in part. But when the consummation comes and what is partial is abolished,"[36] then she will have garments of pure gold. For the garment of rational nature is the "manifold wisdom of God."[37]

*

And so we have come full circle. The foundation of true gnosis is faith, and this faith is always the faith of the Church, compiled by the fathers with the assistance of the Holy Spirit into dogmas in human terms and confessed in baptism. Evagrius knows no other rule. In principle, a "spiritual teacher" who stood outside of this belief and did not preserve unity, would be a heretic.[38] Such a falling away can threaten even those whom Evagrius designates as "authors of true teaching."[39]

What, then, should we make of those who with "vice and false teaching erect"[40] a "tower"[41]? Their alleged "knowledge" is nothing but "error (literally, *not-knowing*) and confusion of the insights,"[42] that is, those things already branded by Paul as "falsely so-called gnosis." He who disseminates it leads others not to true knowledge, but to someone who has become "head of a sect"[43] in the labyrinth of his own confusions. How different is that which the true Christian gnostic does, to whom Evagrius gives the following advice in the last chapter of the little book dedicated to him: "By constantly looking to the Archetype, take pains to draw the 'images,' doing which you should neglect nothing that contributes to restoring a downcast [image]."[44]

The spiritual father, then, is a painter, so to speak, or more precisely a *restorer*, to whom it is entrusted not to "draw" the "image of God" in accordance with his own model, as a copy of himself. Rather, he must take pains to depict it increasingly more like the "original image,"

---

[36]1 Cor 13.9–10.
[37]8 *in Ps* 44.9–10 (citing Eph 3.10).
[38]Cf. the warning about associating with heretics: *Ant. Prol* 6; *Mn* 125, 126; *Gn* 25, 26.
[39]*KG* 4.10, cf. *Gn* 42, 43.
[40]*KG* 4.53.
[41]Cf. Gen 11.4–9.
[42]Ibid. Cf. *in Prov* 30.4: Géhin 282; idem 6.30–31: Géhin 84.
[43]*KG* 5.38.
[44]*Gn* 50.

Christ, until it "resembles"[45] the Lord, as far as is possible in this life. And should one of these "images" (perhaps because defiled by demons) "fall," nevertheless he will "love" it "almost as much as the original image,"[46] since it can never lose this character of the image of God.[47] He will therefore find ways and means to restore it for God, "who wills that all men be saved and come to the knowledge of the truth."[48]

The spiritual father wondrously becomes thereby a co-worker in the salvific work of the heavenly Father, who indeed destined us "from all ages to become equal in form to the image of his Son."[49]

> Grafted into the knowledge of the Lord, the righteous will bring many men to bloom, in this world, that is to say, in the Church, by allowing them to bear fruits through their spiritual teaching.[50]

---

[45] Cf. 18 *in Ps* 88.37–38.
[46] *Pr* 89.
[47] 50 *in Ps* 118.113.
[48] 1 Tim 2.4; cf. *Gn* 22!
[49] *KG* 4.34, cf. Rom 8.29!
[50] 8 *in Ps* 91.14.

Bibliography

[English titles following titles in other languages are provided for information only, and do not refer to actual published translations unless they are introduced by the words, "In English."]

ABBREVIATIONS OF SERIES AND PERIODICALS USED IN THE BIBLIOGRAPHY

CSCO	Corpus Scriptorum Christianorum Orientalium
GCS	Die Griechischen Christlichen Schriftsteller
NPNF	Nicene and Post-Nicene Fathers
OCP	*Orientalia Christiana Periodica*
PG	Patrologia Graeca
PO	Patrologia Orientalis
SC	Sources Chrétiennes
SO	Spiritualité Orientale
TU	Texte und Untersuchungen

WORKS BY EVAGRIUS

Ant   *Antirrhetikos*, ed. by W. Frankenberg, *Evagrius Ponticus*, Berlin (1912): 472–545. Italian trans. by G. Bunge, V. Lazzeri, *Evagrio Pontico, Contro i pensieri malvagi. Antirrhetikos*, Magnano, 2005. [In English, *Talking Back: A Monastic Handbook for Combating Demons*. David Brakke, trans. Collegeville, MN: Liturgical Press, 2009.]

Ep   *Epistulae* (Letters) LXII, ed. W. Frankenberg, loc. cit. German trans. by G. Bunge, Evagrios Pontikos. *Briefe aus der Wüste*, Trier, 1986. Greek fragments in C. Guillaumont, "Fragments grecs inédits d'Évagre le Pontique," TU 133 (1987): 209–221. P. Géhin, "Nouveaux fragments des lettres d'Évagre," *Revue d'Histoire des Textes* 24 (1994): 117–147.

Ep.fid.   *Epistula fidei* (Letter on the Faith). Italian trans. and ed. by J. Bribomont, in M. Forlin-Patrucco, Basilio di Cesarea, *Le lettere*, vol. I, Turin (1983): 84–113. German trans. by G. Bunge,

Briefe, 284–302. [In English, Saint Basil. *The Letters*. R.J. Deferrari, trans. Cambridge, MA: Loeb Classical Library, vol. I, 1926: 47–93.]

Ep.Mel.   *Epistula ad Melaniam*, ed. by Frankenberg, loc. cit.; Part I; G. Vitestam, *Seconde partie du traité, qui passe sous le nome de ‹La grande lettre d'Évagre le Pontique à Mélanie l'Ancienne›* Lund, 1964. [In English, M. Parmentier, trans. "Evagrius of Pontus. Letter to Melania," in *Bijdragen, tijdschrift voor filosofie en theologie* 46 (1985): 2–38; trans. reprinted in *Forms of Devotion: Conversion, Worship, Spirituality, and Asceticism*, ed. by Everett Ferguson, NY: Garland (1999): 272–309.] German trans. by G. Bunge, *Briefe*, 303–328.

Eul   *Tractatus ad Eulogium monachum* (Treatise to Eulogius the Monk). PG 79:1093D–1140A. We follow the text and the numbering of the edition of the better Greek text of the Lavra MS G 93 (E). [In English, *Evagrius of Pontus: The Greek Ascetic Corpus*. R. E. Sinkewicz, ed. and trans. Based on the Greek text of the ms Lavra G 93 (E), Oxford Early Christian Studies, Oxford University Press (2003): 310–333.]

Gn   *Gnostikos* (The Gnostic), ed. and trans. by A. and C. Guillaumont, *Évagre le Pontique. Le Gnostique ou À celui qui est devenu digne de la science*. SC 356, Paris, 1989.

in Eccl   *Scholia in Ecclesiasten* (Scholia on Ecclesiastes), ed. and trans. by P. Géhin, *Évagre le Pontique, Scholies à l'Ecclésiaste*. SC 397, Paris, 1993.

in Prov   *Scholia in Proverbia* (Scholia on Proverbs), ed. and trans. by P. Géhin, *Évagre le Pontique, Scholies aux Proverbes*. SC 340, Paris, 1987.

in Ps   *Scholia in Psalmos* (Scholia on Psalms). With the kind permission of M.J. Rondeau, who is preparing a critical edition of this work on the basis of the MS *Vaticanus Graecus* 754, the collation of which we are using. See also, *id.*, "Le commentaire sur les Psaumes d'Évagre le Pontique," *OCP* 26 (1960): 307–348.

Inst mon   *Institutio ad monachos* (To Monks), PG 79:1236–1240. Suppl. ed. J. Muyldermans, *Evagriana, Le Muséon* 51, Louvain (1938): 198ff.

KG	*Kephalaia Gnostika* (The Gnostic Chapters), ed. and trans. by A. Guillaumont, *Les six Centuries des "Kephalaia Gnostica d'Évagre le Pontique,"* PO 28, Paris, 1958. Greek fragments ed. by J. Muyldermans, *Evagriana*. Extracted from the review *Le Muséon*, vol. XLIV, augmented by: "Nouveaux fragments grecs inédits," Paris (1931); *id.* "*À travers la tradition manuscripte d'Évagre le Pontique,"* in *Bibliothèque du Muséon* 3 (1932); I. Hausherr, "Nouveaux fragments grecs d'Évagre le Pontique," OCP 5 (1939): 229–233. Ch. Furrer-Pilliod, *Horoi kai Hypographai. Coll. Alphabétiques de définitions profanes et sacrées,* in ST 395, 2000. [In English, there is a translation of six of the centuries by David Brundy in *Ascetic Behavior in Greco-Roman Antiquity,* Vincent Wimbush, ed., Minneapolis: Fortress Press (1990): 175–186.]

M.c.	*De diversis malignis cogitationibus* (On Various Evil Thoughts), ed. and trans. by P. Géhin, C. Guillaumont and A. Guillaumont, *Évagre le Pontique, Sur les Pensées,* SC 438, Paris, 1998. [In English, *Evagrius of Pontus: The Greek Ascetic Corpus,* Robert E. Sinkewicz, trans., Oxford Early Christian Studies. NY: Oxford University Press (2003): 136–182. See also *The Philokalia: The Complete Text,* Vol. I, G.E.H. Palmer, Philip Sherrard, and Kallistos Ware, trans., London: Faber & Faber (1971): 38–52] A partial English trans. may be found on pp. 117–124 of *Early Fathers from the Philokalia* by E. Kadloubovsky and G.E.H. Palmer, London: Faber & Faber, 1978.]

Mn	*Sententiae ad monachos* (Sentences for Monks), Hugo Gressmann, ed., *Nonnenspiegel und Mönchsspiegel des Evagrios Pontikos* TU 39, 3 (1913): 143–165. [In English, see *Evagrius Ponticus, Ad Monachos,* trans. by Jeremy Driscoll. Ancient Christian Writers 59. NY: Paulist Press, 2003. See also *The Mind's Long Journey to the Holy Trinity: The* Ad Monachos *of Evagrius Ponticus,* Jeremy Driscoll, trans. Collegeville, MN: Liturgical Press, 1993.]

Or	*De oratione tractatus* (Treatise on Prayer), PG 79:1165A–1200C. J.M. Suarez, S.P.N. Nili Abbatis, *Tractatus seu Opuscula,* Rome (1673): 475–511; the treatise *De oratione* (PG 79:1165A–1200C), and *Philokalia,* vol. I, Athens (1957), 176ff. German trans. *Philokalie der heiligen Väter der Nüchternheit,* vol. I, Würzburg (2004): 287–309. [In English, *The Praktikos: Chapters on Prayer,* John E. Bramberger, trans. Cistercian Studies, Number Four. Spencer,

Massachusetts: Cistercian Publications, 1970. Another trans. may be found on pp. 55–71 of *The Philokalia: The Complete Text*, vol. 1, compiled by St Nikodimos of the Holy Mountain and St Macarius of Corinth, trans. G.E.H. Palmer, Philip Sherrard, and Kallistos Ware. London: Faber & Faber, 1970.]

O.sp. *Tractatus de octo spiritibus malitiae* (On the Eight Spirits of Evil), PG 79:1145A–1164D. German trans. by G. Bunge, *Evagrios Pontikos. Über die acht Gedanken*, Würzburg, 1992. Beuron (2, 2007). We follow the numbering by R. E. Sinkewicz, who took over our numbering and corrected it. [In English, *Evagrius of Pontus: The Greek Ascetic Corpus*, Robert E. Sinkewicz, trans. Oxford Early Christian Studies. NY: Oxford University Press (2003): 66–90.]

Pr *Capita practica ad Anatolium* (Practical Chapters to Anatolius), ed. and trans. by A. and C. Guillaumont, *Évagre le Pontique, Traité pratique ou Le moine*, SC 170–171, Paris, 1971. German trans. with spiritual commentary: G. Bunge, Evagrios Pontikos, *Praktikos oder Der Mönch*, Cologne, 1989. Beuron (2, 2008). [For an English trans. please see above, s.v. *Or.*]

Sent *Sexti Pythagorici, Clitarchi, Evagrii Pontici Sententiae* (Sentences of Sextus Pythagoricus, Clitarchus, and Evagrius Ponticus), ed. by A. Elter, Leipzig, 1892.

Sk *Skemmata* (Reflections), ed. by J. Muyldermans, *Evagriana*, in *Le Muséon* 44, augmented with "Nouveaux fragments grecs inédits," Paris (1931): 38ff. [In English, "The Sapphire Light of the Mind: The *Skemmata* of Evagrius Ponticus," William Harmless and Raymond R. Fitzgerald, trans. in *Theological Studies* 62 (2001): 498–529.]

Vg *Sententiae ad virgines* (Sentences to the Virgins), ed. by Hugo Gressmann, op. cit. [English trans. by Sinkewicz, op. cit., 131–135].

Vit *De vitiis quae opposite sunt virtutibus* (On the Vices that are Opposed to the Virtues), PG 79:1140ff. We follow the Sinkewicz numbering, pp. 60–65. See also *Textverbesserungen* (Text corrections), loc. cit., 293–294.

OTHER SOURCE TEXTS

HL   Palladius, *Historia Lausiaca*, ed. by C. Butler, *The Lausiac History of Palladius*, Cambridge, 1898 and 1904. [For a more recent trans. see Robert T. Meyer, *Palladius: The Lausiac History*, Westminster, MD: Newman Press, 1965. German trans. J. Laager, *Palladius, Historia Lausiaca*, Zürich, 1987.]

HL syr.   Id. *Syriac Version*, ed. and trans. by R. Draguet, *Les formes syriaques de la matière de l'Histoire Lausiaque*, CSCO 389/390 and 398/399, Louvain, 1979.

HE   Sokrates von Konstantinopel, *Kirchengeschichte*, ed. by G.C. Hansen (GCS); trans. by P. Périchon and P. Maraval, SC 477, Paris (2004), SC 493 (2005), SC 505 (2006), SC 506 (2007). [In English, *Socrates of Constantinople*, A.C. Zenos, trans. NPNF, series 2, vol. 2 (1890): 1–178; reprt. Grand Rapids, MI, 1952.]

HE   *Sozomen Church History*, trans. by C.D. Hartranft, NPNF, series 2, vol. 2 (1889): 236–427. Greek text ed. by G.C. Hansen; German trans. by G. C. Hansen, *Fontes Christiani* 73, 1–4, Turnhout, 2004.

HM   *Historia monachorum in Aegypto*, ed. and trans. by A.-J. Festugière, (Subsidia Hagiographica 53), Louvain, 1961.

HM (Rufinus) *Historia monachorum in Aegypto*, ed. by E. Schulz-Flügel, *Tyrannius Rufinus, Historia monachorum, sive De vita sanctorum patrum*, Patristische Texte und Untersuchungen 34, Berlin-New York, 1990. [In English, *The Lives of the Desert Fathers: The "Historia monachorum in Aegypto*," Norman Russell, trans. London: Mowbray and Kalamazoo: Cistercian Publications, 1981]. Italian trans.: G. Trettel, Rufino di Concordia, *Storia dei monaci*, Rome, 1991.

VA   *Vita Antonii*, Athanasius of Alexandria, ed. and trans. by G.J.M. Bartelink, *Athanase d'Alexandrie. Vie d'Antoine*, SC 400, Paris (1994). [In English, *The Life of Antony*, Robert C. Gregg, trans. San Francisco: Harper, 2006.]

Vita   Palladius, *Vita Evagrii coptice*, introduction, trans., and commentary by G. Bunge and A. de Vogüé, *Quatre ermites égyptiens d'après les fragments coptes de l'Histoire Lausiaque*, SO 60, Bellefontaine (1994): 153–175.

Further Evagriana by the Author

"Évagre le Pontique et les deux Macaire," *Irénikon* 56 (1983): 215–227; 323–360.

Akedia. Die geistliche Lehre des Evagrios Pontikos vom Überdruss. Cologne, 1983. 4th edition, Würzburg, 1995. [In English: *Despondency: The Spiritual Teaching of Evagrius Ponticus on Acedia,* Anthony P. Gythiel, trans. Yonkers, NY: St Vladimir's Seminary Press, 2012.]

Evagrios Pontikos. *Briefe aus der Wüste* (Sophia, vol. 24). Trier, 1986.

"Origenissmus–Gnostizismus. Zum geistesgeschichtlichen Standort des Evagrius Pontikos," *Vigiliae Christianae* 40 (1986): 24–54.

"The 'Spiritual Prayer': On the Trinitarian Mysticism of Evagrius of Pontus," *Monastic Studies* 17 (1986): 191–208.

Das Geistgebet: Studien zum Traktat De Oratione *des Evagrios Pontikos* (Koinonia–Oriens, vol. 25). Cologne, 1987.

"'Priez sans cesse.' Aux origins de la prière hésychaste," *Studia Monastica* 30 (1988): 7–16.

Evagrios Pontikos. *Praktikos oder Der Mönch: Hundert Kapitel über das geistliche Leben* (Koinonia–Oriens, vol. 32). Cologne, 1989. Second improved and enhanced edition, Weisungen der Väter, vol. 6. Beuron 2008.

"Hénade ou Monade? Au sujet de deux notions centrales de la terminologie évagrienne." *Le Muséon* 102 (1989): 69–91.

"Mysterium Unitatis. Der Gedanke der Einheit von Schöpfer und Geschöpf in der evagrianischen Mystik." *Freiburger Zeitschrift für Philosophie und Theologie* 36 (1989): 449–469.

"'Nach dem Intellekt leben.' Zum sog. 'Intellektualismus' der evagrianischen Spiritualität," *"Simandrion—Der Wachklopfer." Gedenkenschrift für Klaus Gamber,* ed. by W. Nyssen. Cologne (1989): 95–109.

"Palladiana I. Introduction aux fragments coptes de l'Histoire Lausiaque." *Studia Monastica* 32 (1990): 79–129 (61ff. Évagre et ses amis dans l'Histoire Lausiaque).

With A. de Vogüé: "Palladiana III: La version copte de 'l'Histoire Lausiaque,'" II. "La Vie d'Évagre," *Studia Monastica* 33 (1991): 7–21.

With A. de Vogüé. *Quatre ermites egyptiens: d'après les fragments coptes de Evagrius Pontikos. Über die acht Gedanken,* Würzburg 1992. Second improved edition (Weisungen der Väter 3). Beuron, 2007.

"Der mystische Sinn der Schrift. Anlässlich der Veröffentlichung der Scholien zum Ecclesiasten des Evagrios Pontikos." *Studia Monastica* 36 (1994): 135–146.

"Evagrios Pontikos, hl.," in: Lexikon für Theologie und Kirche, 3rd ed., vol. 3 (1995): col. 1027–1028.

Evagrio Pontico. *Lettere dal deserto.* Introduction and notes by Gabriel Bunge. Trans. from Greek and Syriac by Salvatore di Meglio and Gabriel Bunge. Magnano, 1995.

"Praktikē, Physikē und Theologikē als Stufen der Erkenntnis bei Evagrios Pontikos." *Ab Oriente et Occidente: Gedenkschrift für Wilhelm Nyssen*, ed. by M. Schneider and W. Berschin. St. Ottilien (1996): 59–72.

"'Créé pour être.' A propos d'une citation scripturaire inaperçue dans le 'Peri Archon' d'Origène (3.5.6)," *Bulletin de Littérature Ecclésiastique* 98 (1997): 21–29.

"Evagrios Pontikos: Der Prolog des *Antirrhetikos.*" *Studia Monastica* 39 (1997): 77–105.

"Erschaffen und erneuert nach dem Bilde Gottes. Zu den biblisch-theologischen und sakramentalen Grundlagen der evagrianischen Mystik." *Homo Medietas: Aufsätze zu Religiosität, Literatur und Denkformen des Menschen vom Mittelalter bis in die Neuzeit : Festschrift für Alois Maria Haas zum 65. Geburtstag.* Bern and New York (1999): 27–41.

"Aktive und kontemplative Weise des Betens im Traktat *De Oratione* des Evagrius Pontikos." *Studia Monastica* 41 (1999): 211–227.

Drachenwein und Engelsbrot. Die Lehre des Evagrios Pontikos von Zorn und Sanftmut. Würzburg, 1999. [In English: *Dragon's Wine and Angel's Bread: The Teachings of Evagrius Ponticus on Anger and Meekness,* Anthony P. Gythiel, trans. Crestwood, NY: St Vladimir's Seminary Press, 2009.]

"'La montagne intelligible.' De la contemplation indirecte à la connaissance immédiate de Dieu dans le traité *De Oratione* d'Évagre le Pontique." *Studia Monastica* 42 (2000): 7–26.

"La Gnosis Christou di Evagrio Pontico." In *L'epistula fidei di Evagrio Pontico. Temi, contesti, sviluppi.* Acts of the 3rd Convegno del Gruppo Italiano di Ricerca su "Origene e la Tradizione Alessandrina" (16–19 September 1998). *Studia Ephemeridis Augustinianum* 72 (2000): 153–181.

Evagrio Pontico. *Contro i pensieri malvagi. Antirrhetikos.* Introduction and commentary G. Bunge. Translation V. Lazzeri. Magnano, 2005.

"L'Esprit compatissant. L'Esprit Saint, Maître de la 'prière véritable' dans la spiritualité d'Évagre le Pontique." *Buisson Ardent* 13 (2007): 106–12.